Ira Lois Brown

A FORGE OF
FREEDOM BOOK

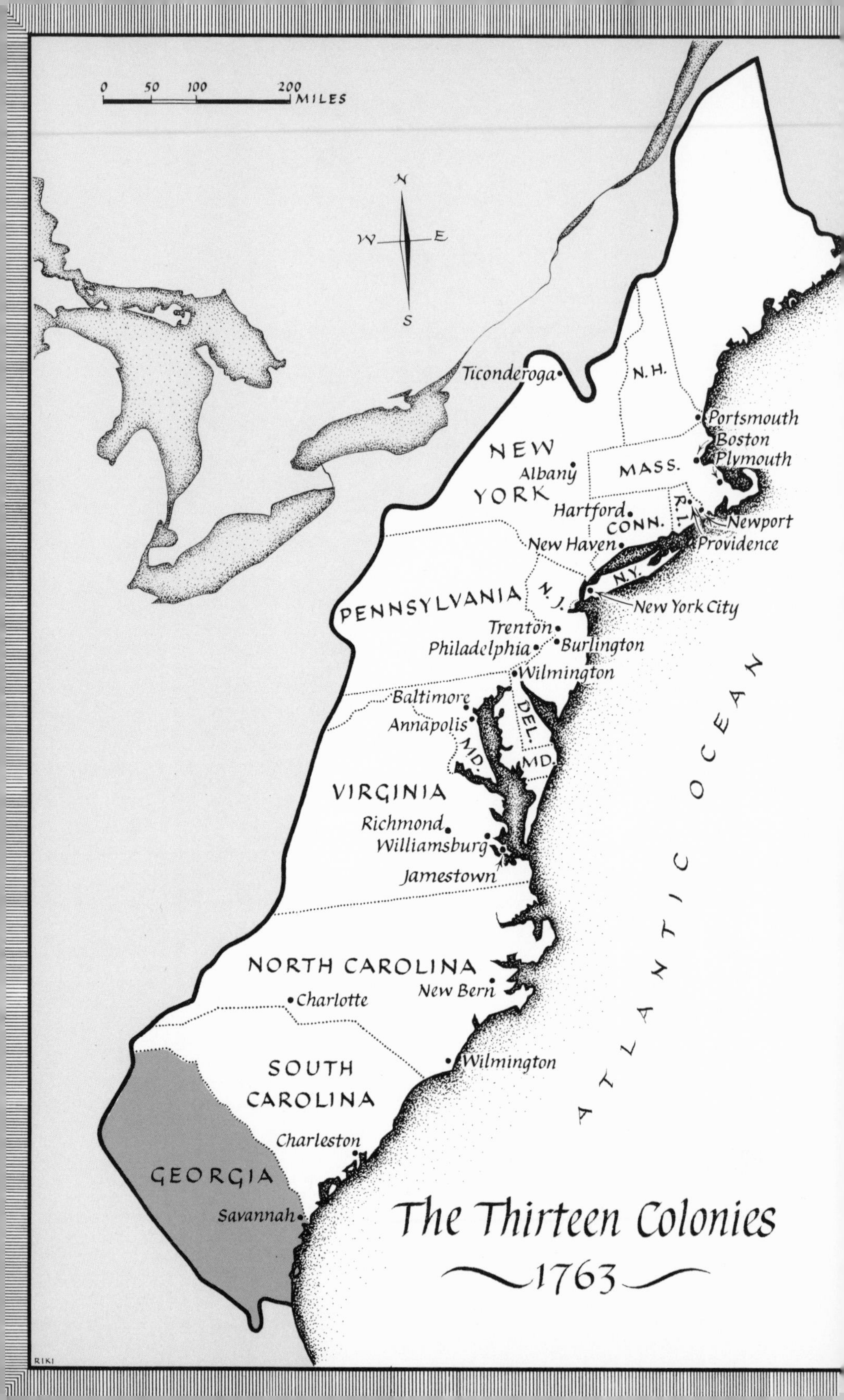

0 50 100 200 MILES
N
W E
S
Ticonderoga
N.H.
Portsmouth
Boston
Plymouth
NEW YORK
Albany
MASS.
Hartford
R.I.
CONN.
Newport
New Haven
Providence
N.Y.
N.J.
New York City
PENNSYLVANIA
Trenton
Philadelphia
Burlington
Wilmington
Baltimore
Annapolis
DEL.
MD.
MD.
VIRGINIA
Richmond
Williamsburg
Jamestown
ATLANTIC OCEAN
NORTH CAROLINA
New Bern
Charlotte
Wilmington
SOUTH CAROLINA
Charleston
GEORGIA
Savannah
The Thirteen Colonies
1763
RIKI

THE GEORGIA COLONY

by

Ira L. Brown

CROWELL-COLLIER PRESS
Collier-Macmillan Limited / London

To all the people who have lived our history,
to those who have treasured and made known our heritage
and to those who believe that all things are possible

Library of Congress Catalog Card Number: 73–95174

The Macmillan Company
866 Third Avenue
New York, New York 10022
Collier-Macmillan Canada Ltd., Toronto, Ontario

Printed in the United States of America
FIRST PRINTING

Culver Pictures, Inc., 16, 23, 35, 61; Historical Pictures Service—Chicago, 4, 9, 25, 38, 46, 49, 51, 65, 66–67, 69, 78, 94, 104, 107; North Carolina Collection, 36; Radio Times Hulton Picture Library, 2, 7, 13.

JACKET ILLUSTRATION: *The Spanish invasion of 1742*

Contents

Why a Thirteenth Colony? 1

The new colony was the talk of London that summer of 1732. Newspapers like the *Daily Journal* and the *Grub Street Journal,* and magazines like the *London Magazine* and the *Gentleman's Magazine,* carried news and articles about it. This new colony would be south of the Carolinas and it was to be named Georgia, after His Majesty King George II. The English had started no colony in the southeastern part of America since South Carolina was founded in 1670. Georgia was to be different from all the other colonies for the settlers were to be chosen from the "industrious yet unfortunate poor" of England and to include "foreigners persecuted for conscience sake."

The London public already knew who was to manage the new colony. A twenty-one-man corporation called the Trustees for Establishing the Colony of Georgia in America had been appointed by the King and given a charter for twenty-one years. The charter granted them the land between the Savannah and Altamaha rivers and "Westerly from the said rivers respectively in direct line to the South Seas." The fact that Spain and France might also claim

King George II of England, for whom the colony of Georgia was named.

some of this enormous grant of land did not bother King George. It was good news to the people of London to hear of a new colony and new opportunities. They were very impressed with these Trustees who would work without pay and without profit or reward. Everyone was eager to hear more about Georgia and the Trustees' plans.

Londoners knew that times were hard and that a great many people were out of work, poor and hungry. These idle workers might have gone to America if they had been able to pay the fare. Generally, if a person with no money wished to go to America, he could agree to work as a servant for a certain number of years for the person who paid his fare. This new colony was not only asking for jobless people to come and settle, but the Trustees would pay their way if accepted. They were also to receive a grant of land and a year's support of food and supplies. They would not be indentured servants to the Trustees but free English citizens owning their own land.

This was good news indeed, and London boys like John Goddard, Charles Clark and Marmaduke Cannon probably listened for more tidings as they wandered through the bustling, noisy streets. It would be a good report to take home to worried parents. Families like the Cannons and the Clarks had new babies and no money. Here was a chance for a new life. The boys might have heard more gossip among the merchants on the porch of the Church of St. Mary le Bow in Cheapside, the same church whose Bow bells called Dick Whittington back to London. They could have heard it in the many taverns or coffee houses. Here the men of London gathered to talk and exchange news. One of them might occasionally want a message delivered by an enterprising boy for a penny or a halfpenny. The boys' mothers might have heard about Georgia in church. In many parishes sermons were being preached in praise of the new colony and Trustees such as James Oglethorpe, Lord Percival and Thomas Coram.

Churches were collecting money to help with the new venture. From all over England leading citizens were asking for commissions from the Trustees to collect funds for the colony. This money would be used by the Trustees for fares, food, clothing and supplies for the worthy and oppressed poor to settle in Georgia. Many people gave donations of money and materials to the popular cause.

Londoners who had kept up with the news for several years would not have been surprised to see James Oglethorpe's name on the Trustee list. They would remember him as being a friend of the poor and those in trouble. Only a few years before, Oglethorpe had been head of a committee to inspect the London prisons where terrible conditions existed. At that time a man could be thrown into jail for debt and kept there until the debt was paid. Since there was no way to earn money in jail, he could not get out unless someone else paid off his debt. The prisons

were dirty, damp, cold and crowded. Food was poor and diseases such as smallpox and tuberculosis were common. Prisoners were often mistreated by cruel and inhumane jailers. These jailers dealt out severe physical punishments, extorted what money the prisoners had, and allowed terrible sanitary conditions. Such neglect and abuse resulted in the death of one of Oglethorpe's friends, the architect Robert Castell, a victim of smallpox in debtor's prison. After learning of his friend's shocking death, Oglethorpe decided he must do something about the jails.

Through his efforts as a member of Parliament, he was made chairman of a committee to investigate prison conditions. As a result of the committee's report, some jailers were tried in court and thousands of debtors were released from prison. Many of these people could not find work after they were released and added to the number of jobless poor of London. Oglethorpe, aware of their problems, was one of the leaders in a new effort to give opportunities to the needy. He had planned and talked with influential friends for several years about a new colony before the king approved their plans and placed his signature on the charter.

Why was this particular region of America chosen when there were other areas claimed by the English which were also not yet settled? And how were Oglethorpe, Lord Percival, James Vernon and other leaders who became Trustees able to get their plans approved? It was not easy to convince the practical men in Parliament, King George II and his ministers that they should grant land and money for the new colony. Some objected that England needed all the population at home to work. Others thought Parliament should not have any power over a colony, only the king and

Hard times in mid-eighteenth century London are depicted in this engraving by Gustave Doré.

those he appointed. It was not the first time that a new colony named Georgia had been proposed. Nor was it the first time a plan had been drawn up to settle the area below the Savannah River. But there were several practical reasons in addition to the charitable one for founding a colony south of Charleston and Beaufort, South Carolina.

That area has been called the Debatable Land because it was claimed by Spain and France as well as England. The Indians regarded it as theirs because they already occupied it and they had proved they could be unfriendly and dangerous in defense of their land. Spanish settlements in St. Augustine and other parts of Florida were near enough to be a continual danger to Charleston. The French and Spanish were busy stirring up the Indians against the English. Thus South Carolina was willing to give up a large part of its original grant in return for some protection from its enemies to the south. The British government wanted to reinforce its claim by settling the land permanently while at the same time providing some defense for the Carolinas.

Another very important reason for establishing the colony appealed especially to the financial and trade interests in Parliament. They thought it would provide a new source of raw materials. The idea of sending jobless people to a new colony and employing them in the production of silk, hemp, wine and other needed goods was a convincing one. It helped solve the unemployment problem at home and at the same time promised new wealth. The Georgia Trustees were highly regarded in Parliament and their arguments were considered reasonable.

Who were the twenty-one "right trusty, and well beloved" men named in the charter as Trustees for Establishing the Colony of Georgia in America when it was finally approved on June 9, 1732? We have already mentioned Lord Percival, who was named first president of

A wretched victim of the intolerable prison conditions crouches before a committee appointed to investigate the atrocities.

the new corporation. He was influential in getting the colony started and he continued to be a leader to whom the colonists and the other Trustees looked. He kept a journal and a diary which are very interesting sources of information about early Georgia. He was a member of Parliament and a good friend of Oglethorpe. He was later made the Earl of Egmont.

James Vernon was also a close friend of Oglethorpe. He was a government official and tax commissioner, and he was known to be modest, sober and well educated. The Reverend Stephen Hales, often referred to as Dr. Hales, was a well-known scientist and naturalist who experimented in botany and chemistry and wrote on these subjects. He was very helpful in raising money for the Trustees to use for the colony.

James Oglethorpe was a member of Parliament as well as a leader in efforts for prison reform. He had been a soldier in the British and foreign armies, which gave him valuable experience for planning the military defense of Georgia and Carolina. Sir Thomas Coram was a sea captain who, like Oglethorpe, was interested in helping people in distress, especially children. He and his wife began the Foundling Hospital in London for orphans. The land he gave is called Coram's Fields, and even today there is a children's playground on it. Other Trustees were clergymen or members of other professions and more than half of them were members of Parliament.

July 20, 1732, was a very important day for all future Georgians. On that day the Trustees held their first meeting after the charter had been granted. It took place in the Palace Court, Old Palace Yard, which was near the Parliament buildings on the Thames River. The Trustees chose a smaller group of their number which was called the Common Council. The Common Council met frequently and did much of the work of the Trustees. There was much to be done. Records had to be kept of all donations received, and committees were appointed for special tasks. One such task was advertising in the newspapers to inform people about the new colony of Georgia. The Trustees also had to approve and commission those people who wished to collect money for them. Another very important task was selecting the new colonists.

There are no records showing exactly how the colonists were selected, but one journal was kept of the meetings of the Trustees and another of the Common Council meetings. These are now a part of the colonial records of Georgia. From time to time a notation in the journals says, "Examined several persons who offered themselves to go to Georgia, and entered their names for further consideration." It seems plenty of people wanted a chance for a new life. In September, 1732, one of the newspapers reported that already more than six hundred people had registered to go to Georgia.

Besides those whose passage would be paid by the Trustees, there were other colonists who would pay their own passage and receive larger grants of land. These people were called adventurers, but it seems accurate to use that term for all the new colonists for they were all about to begin a true adventure. The journal of the Trustees also mentions the Swiss Protestants who settled at Purrysburg in South Carolina, and the Salzburgers, German-speaking Protestants from the Archbishopric of Salzburg in the Holy Roman Empire. Money was donated to help both groups. Later other foreigners would be helped to come to Georgia.

Lists were kept of the early settlers who went to Georgia in the first few years. Among the names are those of many

The Salzburgers leaving their homes for the journey to Georgia.

Londoners, such as Sam Cunningham, a coalseller from Little St. Martin's Lane; Will Curtis, a leather dresser from Warwick Lane; Jo Lawrence, a bookbinder of St. Paul's Churchyard. And the Trustees must have welcomed useful trades like those of Richard Hughes, blacksmith, of Swan Court; David Snook, baker, of Drury Lane; and James Slade, shoemaker, of Shepherd Street, Hanover Square. Since the Trustees met in the Palace Court of Westminster, one can guess it was easy for Hugh Frazer, tailor, of the Stable Yard, Westminster, and Jo Desborough, carpenter, of the same address to hear the news and get on the register of new colonists.

We have no list of the requirements for being a new colonist but we know they were carefully examined and chosen. Most of them were recommended by their parish clergy, and if they had any obligations in London they could not go unless they were relieved or excused of them. From time to time in the journal of the Trustees there are entries about people who were dropped from the list because of a debt or other obligation. No known fugitives from justice were on the first shiploads of future Georgians, only needy and adventurous people.

There was still much to be done before the first embarkation but James Oglethorpe was anxious to begin the work of building the new colony. In the minutes of the Common Council we find this entry for October 3, 1732: "That an Imbarkation not exceeding Thirty five Men and their Familys be made for Georgia upon the Charity received by the Trustees. . . . That 300 pounds be lodged in Mr. Heathcote's hands for the said Purposes. . . . Ordered that Lord Carpenter, Mr. Oglethorpe, Mr. Heathcote, Mr. Hucks, Mr. More, Mr. Tower, Mr. Belitha and Mr. Hales or any Two of them do Treat with proper Persons for carrying on the said Imbarkation."

James Oglethorpe's dream was about to come true.

From Cold London Streets  2

There must have been many disappointed people after the Trustees had notified the people selected to embark on the first shipload to Georgia. Many applicants who had been accepted had to await a later voyage. The Trustees announced that only thirty-five men and their families could depart on the first voyage. There was not yet enough preparation or money for more. Those chosen as colonists were summoned to attend an important meeting of the Trustees Common Council at four o'clock in the afternoon of October 24, 1732. These were people who would soon be important to each other. For the first time they would all meet together.

Probably many of them had already been to the Trustees' office in Westminster. They had found their way to that room in a lane "that goes out of that street that leads from Palace Yard to Milbank Ferry." They would have noted the maps on the office wall but at this particular meeting all must have looked with great interest at the map of the Province of Carolina. The colonists listened while the Articles of Agreement were read to them. Here is a summary of the articles.

1. The new colonists were to regard themselves as soldiers as well as planters. They would be given arms to defend the colony. They would also be given a grant of land and seeds and tools to cultivate it.
2. Those having their passage and provisions paid for by the Trustees were to have a grant of land of 50 acres. This land could be inherited only by a male heir and could not be sold or mortgaged. The colonists who could pay their way could be granted as much as five hundred acres if they brought their own servants.
3. After the colonists arrived in Georgia, a certain amount of time would be given them to clear and cultivate a certain portion of their land. One hundred white mulberry trees had to be planted upon every ten acres cleared. This rule was to encourage the making of raw silk. Silkworms ate white mulberry leaves.
4. The colonists were to agree to obey the rules and laws the Trustees would make. They would stay at least three years in the colony. They would help each other in clearing their lots. For a time, until their own land was cleared and cultivated, they could have provisions from the Trustees store.
5. Rum was forbidden in the colony. They were forbidden to have Negro slaves in the colony. They could not trade with the Indians except by a special permit from the Trustees.

At a second meeting a week later, the new settlers learned that James Oglethorpe himself would accompany them to Georgia. The Trustees were very pleased about this. The colonists would need, as Lord Percival said, "a proper governor" to guide and direct them. Oglethorpe would go entirely at his own expense, as would the Reverend Henry Herbert, a Church of England minister. Dr. William Cox agreed to serve as their physician for a year without charging fees. Three such guides and helpers must have made the settlers feel more confident of their future as they prepared to go aboard the good ship *Ann*.

In accordance with the agreement each colonist signed, the men began receiving military training in order to be ready to defend the new colony from Indians and Spaniards and all enemies. The women packed their meager belongings and said goodbye to friends and relatives. It is likely that the children who were going were the most excited and least worried. They too were having a last look at London. Their new environment would be a profound change.

Only thirty-five men and their families were chosen by the Trustees to embark on the first vessel to Georgia.

They were leaving one of the greatest cities of eighteenth-century Europe. Although there was no census at the time, the estimated population of the city was five hundred thousand, crowded on both sides of the Thames River. It was a busy seaport. Daniel Defoe, the author of *Robinson Crusoe,* counted the ships in the Thames River one day in the early eighteenth century. He claimed to have counted over two thousand sail of all types, not including barges, pleasure boats and yachts, in the Pool of London. At that time a boat trip on the Thames was the best and cheapest way to get from one part of the city to another. There was only one bridge over the river, old London Bridge, which was full of shops and houses. Stairs went down to the water all along the river. At these places one could hire a boat to any point on the river. Most of the boats were small and used oars but larger ones might have a sail also. These larger boats made regular trips down to the town of Gravesend, where passengers could board ships to foreign ports.

London was a cold city. Foreign visitors complained of the thick black fogs and the coal smoke but they were glad for the warm coal fires. It was a crowded city. The streets were narrow and full of carts, wagons, coaches, sedan chairs, men on horseback and pedestrians. In the winter the population was much larger because many wealthier people who lived in other parts of England came to London for the winter. There were so many things to do there during what was called "the season." In the summer many native Londoners who could afford it went to the country.

London was a busy city. Most of the trade of England was conducted there. London had many fine shops brightly lit by candles in the evenings. In these shops you could buy the finest goods in Europe. The streets were lined overhead with huge shop signs. A large picture was painted on each sign to show what kind of shop it was since some of the porters and coachmen could not read.

It was a noisy city. The huge signs creaked and banged in the wind. All day and evening, street sellers called out their wares at the top of their voices: "Chairs to mend, chairs to mend; mackerel, fresh mackerel; rags, any old rags"; or "Ripe strawberries, ripe; hot spice cakes, hot." At every hour of the night a watchman cried out the time in the dark streets. One would hear, "Twelve o'clock, look out for your lock, your fire and your light, and so good night."

London was a city of the very rich and the very poor. It was the home of the wealthy merchant and the tradesman with rising fortune. Thousands were jobless, sick, poor and starving, and crime was widespread. But London was also the home of the king and queen and well-known nobility. It was a cruel city. People flocked to public hangings, bearbaitings and cockfights. Children were abandoned and left to starve. But London was also a cultured and humane city. There were great churches and theaters, concerts and plays. The famous composer Handel was a London hero but all the people hummed tunes from John Gay's *The Beggar's Opera.* The great artist Hogarth was painting London as he saw it. Many hospitals were built for sick people, and schools were set up for orphans. Like Captain Coram, many people wanted to help the distressed, as is proved by the large number of donations to the Georgia Trustees.

London was a dirty city. Mud and filth ran in the gutters and people threw their garbage in the street. But the people loved parks and gardens, bright clothes and white stockings. Fresh water was pumped all over the city in wooden pipes. There were fine houses but many of the poor lived in broken-down houses and damp, cold and smelly basements. Just like many cities today, London was a city of contrasts, and the new colonists must have had mixed feelings about leaving it.

James Oglethorpe was a strong and humane leader.

Their new leader James Oglethorpe was a soldier with a good military reputation. When a very young man he had fought with Prince Eugene of Savoy against the Turks. His family home was at Godalming in the County of Surrey, England. His father, Sir Theophilus Oglethorpe and his mother, Lady Eleanor, had faithfully served the Stuart royal family of England before King George I and the Hanover family became England's ruling family. A few years after Oglethorpe's return from service with Prince Eugene, he was elected to Parliament. He was an active, fair-minded member who favored the best interests of the majority rather than an elite few. He was a witty and eloquent speaker, "a gentleman of unblemished character, brave, generous and humane," as well as handsome and well educated. He was, besides, a strong leader, interested in the welfare of the underprivileged, and sensitive to the problems of individuals.

By November 16, 1732, everything was ready for the first embarkation. The ship *Ann,* a galley of two hundred tons, with Captain John Thomas and its crew was anchored at Gravesend. The passengers, provisions and baggage were aboard. A few of the Trustees made a special trip to Gravesend with Oglethorpe and Dr. Herbert. They came aboard and met with the colonists in the great cabin. The passenger roll was called and a few last-minute matters were settled.

The colonists presented a petition thanking the Trustees for all their favors and labors in their behalf. The Trustees inspected the accommodations and were satisfied that all was in order. When they found there was a new baby aboard who had not yet been christened, they provided two guineas to buy supplies for the christening party. They then said their farewells to Oglethorpe and the new settlers. That same evening the *Ann* fell farther down the river toward the English Channel.

To Southern Pine Forests 3

Safe on board the *Ann* with a long voyage ahead the passengers had ample time to get to know each other. Some would be given tasks and positions of responsibility which would greatly affect the new colony. To two of these first settlers, Thomas Christie and Peter Gordon, we owe much of what we know about the voyage. They both kept a brief record of it.

Thomas Christie had been a merchant and was made recorder of the new colony. Peter Gordon was an upholsterer and was among the first to be appointed a bailiff, a civil officer. Thomas Causton had been a calico printer and he too was appointed a bailiff. His most important job in Georgia was as keeper of the Trustees' public store. Joseph Fitzwalter had been a gardener and became a constable and public gardener in Georgia. Paul Amatis was an Italian silk expert. He came expressly because of this knowledge and was to have charge of the silk industry and be the public gardener. Noble Jones had been a carpenter and became surveyor, constable and many other things in Georgia. It is because of the care and forethought of his descendants that we have so much material on early Georgia. The following occupations were listed by other passengers: smith, tailor, wigmaker, baker, writer, farmer, stocking maker, flax and hemp dresser, apothecary, vintner, sawyer, wheelwright and cloth merchant.

There were plenty of children aboard the ship. James Goddard, Charles Clark and Marmaduke Cannon have already been mentioned. Other boys from nine to twelve years old were John Milledge, James Thibaut and young Noble Wimberly Jones. Girls of the same age group were Sarah Milledge, Mary Cormock and Elizabeth Wright. There were some twenty younger children and babies and a dozen or so young people in their teens including Robert Johnson and Samuel Parker, Jr., and the sisters Mary and Elizabeth Hodges. *The Gentlemen's Magazine* reported in November, 1732, that some couples aboard the *Ann* had already promised marriage "so the Reverend Dr. Herbert will not be without employment."

It must have been crowded aboard ship. The people slept in wooden cradles which were five feet eight inches long inside. Someone kept watch every night to see there were no fires and to help any sick people. In addition to people and supplies, there were animals aboard ship: hogs, sheep, ducks, geese and several dogs, including one belonging to Oglethorpe that was lost at sea. We can guess that the older children helped look after the animals and watched over the younger children.

Thomas Christie reported that every Thursday and Sunday the passengers had pork and peas to eat. On Saturday they had stockfish with butter and every other day, beef and suet pudding. They ate carrots and potatoes and had onions once a week. There was bread and beer for all passengers. At that time most English people, children as well as adults, drank some kind of beer. It was probably much like cider. There was sage tea, water gruel with sugar, and white wine for the sick. Oglethorpe would send fresh broth made from his own food supplies for the sick. Much of the food was salted or dried since most of the meat had to be preserved in this way. Water was kept in barrels and was not plentiful.

Oglethorpe, Dr. Herbert and Dr. Cox frequently visited the passengers in their quarters, especially the sick. When Oglethorpe caught a large fish he gave it all to the women passengers. One account tells of a calm day when he, Dr. Herbert, Captain Thomas and some others went fishing in the longboat using umbrellas to protect themselves from the hot sun.

Every Sunday Dr. Herbert held a religious service, "prayers and a sermon." Sometimes this was in the great cabin and sometimes on deck in good weather. There were several special occasions, among them the christening of the new baby named Georgius Marinus Warren. According to Peter Gordon, there was merriment after the baptism and plenty of flip, a sweetened mixture of beer and spices, for everyone. By the time they celebrated Oglethorpe's birthday on December 21, the ship was quite far south and the weather was hot. On that occasion there was mutton and broth for dinner and plenty of punch to drink. Afterwards there were deck games like cudgel-playing, the art of defense with heavy clubs. Christmas was celebrated in "exceedingly hot weather." There were prayers and a sermon by Dr. Herbert. For dinner there was mutton, broth, pudding and flip to drink.

People were seasick but no one was seriously ill on the voyage except two infants. James Cannon and James Clark, both less than a year old, died aboard ship and were buried at sea. Oglethorpe wrote the Trustees that the babies were half-starved and weak when they came aboard. Sunshine, sea air and freedom from worry about food and shelter must have been good for the other passengers.

After two months at sea everyone aboard welcomed the sight of landbirds promising the end of the voyage. According to Peter Gordon's journal, "Jan. the 13th about nine in the morning we see two sails of shipps, and soon after we made land and stood for it, which we discovered in a short time to be Charles Town." Thomas Christie hastened to send his record of the voyage by a ship bound for London. He sent it to Trustee Thomas Tower and begged him to "put up a Thanksgiving for our safe passage."

The *Ann* anchored some distance from Charleston for the colonists were not to land there. Oglethorpe went ashore to consult and be welcomed by South Carolina's Governor Robert Johnson while the passengers on the *Ann* fished for their dinners with great success. By night Mr. Oglethorpe returned aboard and the ship sailed south for Port Royal. There the barracks at the fort had been prepared for the colonists until enough boats could be gathered for their trip to Georgia.

Not many new settlers in America received such a gracious welcome as these new Georgia colonists did from the people of South Carolina. Peter Gordon wrote in his journal: "About noon, we were all safely landed at the new fort where we found . . . the barracks . . . clean'd out on purpose for our reception, fires lighted, and provisions provided for our refreshment. During our stay here, which was ten days, we were constantly visited by the planters of the country and diverted ourselves with fishing and shooting." The town of Beaufort was quite near and some of the colonists visited it and were well entertained.

Meanwhile Oglethorpe and Colonel William Bull of South Carolina, "a gentleman of great experience in making settlements," had gone to select the site of the new town on the Savannah River. This was only the beginning of Colonel Bull's services to the new colony. They selected a site on a high bluff on the river about eighteen miles from the Atlantic to be called the new town of Savannah. Oglethorpe wrote the Trustees: "The river here forms a half-moon, along the south side of which the banks are about 40 feet high, and on the top a flat, which they call a bluff. The plain high ground extends into the country about 5 or 6 miles, and along the river about a mile. Ships that draw 12 feet of water can ride within ten yards of the bank. . . .The river is pretty wide, the water fresh, and from the Key . . . you see its whole course to the sea, with the Island of Tybee, which forms the Mouth of the River; and the other way you see the River for about six miles up into the Country. The Landskip is very agreeable, the Stream being wide, and border'd with high woods on both sides."

Before deciding on this site for Savannah, it was necessary to get the permission of the Indians. A small tribe of Yamacraw Indians had their village nearby. Oglethorpe visited the village and met Tomo-chi-chi, their chief. Through an interpreter, Oglethorpe persuaded Tomo-chi-chi that the colonists were friendly and the chief gave his permission.

When Oglethorpe returned to Port Royal a day of thanksgiving was held. The South Carolinians in Beaufort and Port Royal joined the colonists in prayers and then a feast. By that time enough boats had been gathered to transport the settlers to their new home. South Carolina furnished a sloop and five periaguas (a type of flat boat) to carry them and their belongings. For safety in their smaller boats they followed inland coastal water passages. As Oglethorpe had planned, they camped overnight on Jones Island where a troop of Rangers, brave frontier soldiers, had made huts in which they spent the night. Indian hunters provided venison.

On February 12, by our present calendar, the colonists reached Yamacraw Bluff. There was no time to lose if they were to have shelter for the night. They began to unload their goods and set up tents. Soon after landing the colonists had their first look at their new neighbors, the Yamacraw Indians. Tomo-chi-chi, who would prove their true and noble friend, came to welcome them.

Thomas Causton described the meeting in a letter home: "Before them [the Indians] came a man dancing in antick postures with a spread of white feathers in each hand as a token of friendship." Causton continues to describe the fans as attached to long rods set with small bells. The dancer jingled the bells and the Indians made a "hollowing" (loud calls of greeting) . Oglethorpe greeted them and the dancer spoke of their warriors' brave deeds. While doing this he waved his fans and sometimes stroked Oglethorpe with them. Causton continues, "Then the King [Tomo-chi-chi] and all the men came in a regular manner and shook him by the hand. After that the Queen came and all the women did the like. Then Mr. Oglethorpe conducted them to his tent and made them sit down."

Oglethorpe and his expedition selected a site on the Savannah River for the new town of Savannah.

Oglethorpe arranged with the Yamacraw hunters to furnish fresh game, venison and turkeys, while the colonists were busy with urgent work. For some time the first Georgians lived in large tents. When there were heavy rains the tents leaked and the settlers had to cover their beds with bowls, cups and plates to catch the water. Perhaps they used the wooden bowls given out to every family the first week together with an iron pot, frying pan, a Bible and a Book of Common Prayer.

There were many jobs to be done. The trees must be cleared from the land. Timber must be prepared to build houses and a palisade fence to protect the settlement. Men were needed to build a crane to lift goods from the river to the high bluff. If they were to have vegetables and grain the land must be prepared and seeds planted.

Governor Johnson and the Council of South Carolina gave a hundred head of cattle, two dozen hogs and twenty barrels of rice to the new colonists. Mr. Whitaker and friends gave another hundred head of cattle. Other South Carolinians sent sheep and horses. A company of Rangers and a scout boat helped with many tasks. Colonel Bull came back to Georgia and brought four Negro sawyers who were much needed. Mr. Joseph Bryan and Mr. Barlow came and brought servants to help. Mr. St. Julien spent several weeks directing the building.

Oglethorpe and Colonel Bull had planned the town. One of Savannah's early inhabitants described Savannah as beautifully laid out with public squares left at proper distances for markets and public buildings. If necessary the squares were to be used for outlying settlers to camp on in case of wars or Indian uprisings. Savannah's main street was named Bull Street and its first square Johnson Square in honor of their Carolina friends. In a little more than a week the first house was begun. From the beginning the men had guard duty and a guard house was built on the river. A look-

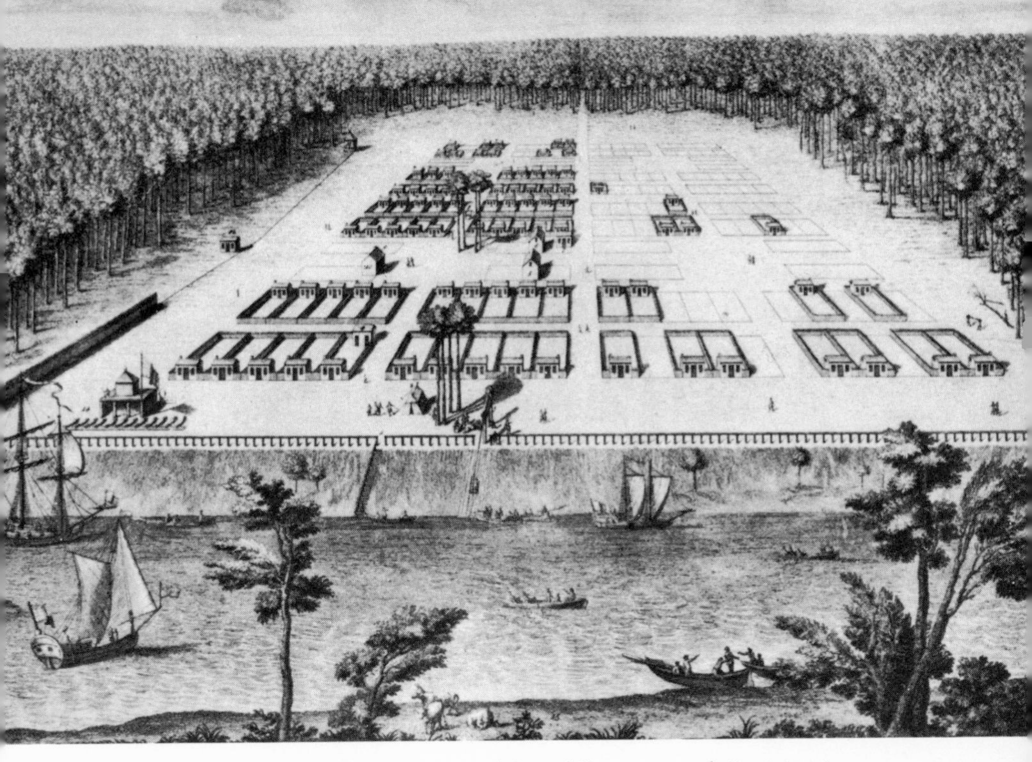

Savannah was beautifully laid out with public squares left at proper distances for markets and public buildings.

out was always kept there and guns were mounted to protect the river approaches.

A visitor from South Carolina described the new settlement in late March. He spoke of Oglethorpe's work and care of all the people: "He is extremely well beloved by all his People; the general title they give him is Father. . . . There are no idlers there; even the boys and girls do their part." He spoke of four houses already up but none finished, and several gardens planted. He continues, "In short he has done a vast deal of work for the time and I think his name justly deserves to be immortalized."

This optimism was shared by the colonists themselves. Thomas Causton, Georgia's new keeper of the Trustees' public store, wrote cheerfully to his wife in London, "There is no room to doubt we shall be a flourishing people and hope to be 1,000 strong by the years end."

Mistress Georgia, How Does Your Garden Grow?

4

Any time human beings move from one place to another, the first thing they must do is look after two basic needs. They must have food and shelter—protection from starvation, the weather and danger. Providing food and shelter were the two things that kept the new colonists busy for some time. What they had to do to provide these basic needs depended almost entirely on the climate, soil, plants and animals already in Georgia. It also depended on whether the Indians who lived there were friends or enemies. This colony had been written and talked about so much in England. It is interesting to examine how well the descriptions of it fitted the way the colonists found it.

We know that the Trustees' plan for colonizing Georgia was not the first plan for settling that part of America. In 1717 Sir Robert Montgomery had a very fine-sounding plan for a colony there. He had written and published a pamphlet describing this proposed colony "in the most delightful country of the Universe." He also claimed that "nature has not blessed the world with any tract which can be preferable to it," that "Paradise may be supposed at most but equal to its native excellencies." Sir Robert thought that settlers there could quickly expect wealth, safety and liberty. These impractical ideas and the laziness shown by some of the colonists tell us one important fact—that few people in England of any class, rich or poor, understood the back-breaking work it took to establish a new colony in the wilderness.

Later, in 1732, another pamphlet describing Georgia was circulated in London. This pamphlet also praised the temperature, climate and natural healthiness of the country. The land was reported to be so fertile that crops would increase one hundred fold. A poem told of the natural beauty and fruits found there, describing blossoms and ripe fruit growing on the same tree and spring-like weather all year. Here are the last four lines:

> So sweet the air, so moderate the clime
> None sickly lives or dies before his time
> Heav'n sure has kept this spot of earth uncurs't
> To show how all things were created first.

All this enthusiasm was not completely without reason. Some of the statements were true but only in certain places and at certain times. The soil in some places was very fertile, as a number of fortunate colonists discovered. But much of the soil around Savannah was sandy and not by its nature good for growing things. Even the native Indians had found it was necessary to fertilize their crops. Many hands were needed to plant, tend and gather the crops, and in the early days of the colony this was all hand labor.

Oglethorpe himself, after more than a year in the colony, gave the following description in a letter to Samuel Wesley, whose son John was considering coming to Georgia: "There are not only the hazards and inconveniences of a sea passage . . . but when he arrives he must be prepared to meet with differences of climate." Oglethorpe mentioned the lack of all luxuries and sometimes of necessities. He spoke of the air being clearer and more piercing; of the heat in summer being greater but the shorter winter's cold less raw; of gnats and flies and little red vermin or lice. He described the thunder and lightning and violent showers. These, he said, cause a "fragrancy superior to the most blooming spring in Europe."

The contrast in climate between England and Georgia was very great and it had a very serious effect on many of the early colonists. It often brought illness and all newcomers went through an adjustment. The older colonists called it "seasoning" and expected illness or weakness until the newcomer became used to the different climate.

There is a great difference between England and Georgia in the distance from the equator. Savannah, Georgia, is situated about thirty-two degrees latitude, which is about the same as that of Jerusalem and near that of Cairo, Egypt. London's latitude is about the same as Labrador's in northern Canada. Probably even harder than the change in location was the adjustment to the great and rapid contrasts in Georgia weather itself. The temperature in England is not nearly so variable.

William Stephens, the Trustees' secretary who was later appointed president, kept a journal for several years on his stay in Georgia. He frequently mentioned the rapid changes of the weather and commented once that the change in temperature in one day was equal to that between summer and winter in England. Snow was not unknown though very rare. Stephens described a snowfall on November 25, 1740, which had reached four or five inches by ten o'clock in the morning but began to melt and was almost gone by noon. Though rainfall is plentiful in England, there are seldom heavy and violent rainstorms as in Georgia.

One of the best accounts of the geography of this part

of Georgia was given by William Bartram, a naturalist who visited Georgia before the Revolutionary War. He described the land from a journey he made from Savannah to Augusta as follows. The first fifty miles from the coast was level plain and loose sandy soil where grew pine, oak, tulip, sweet gum, mulberry, redbud, basswood, swamp cottonwood, sycamore, sassafras, bay, white ash, elm, hickory and silverbell trees. One third of this region was swampland. Here grew cypress trees, the beautiful magnolia and swamp azalea and many palmetto trees. In the trees grew vines of American wisteria, trumpet flowers and honeysuckle. The swampy soil he described as fertile.

According to Bartram a gradual climb of eight or ten miles led to a gently rising plain about seventy miles wide. This plain was grass-covered and dotted with many ponds. On it grew evergreen trees such as pine, magnolia and holly plus many other trees already mentioned. The soil he described as light sandy loam over clay. The next level plain came after a broken rise of ten or fifteen miles. It had much the same vegetation and trees though the soil there was dusky brown color over clay.

Until their crops grew, the colonists depended for part of their food on the native birds, animals and fish. In 1739 one of Oglethorpe's frontier soldiers accompanied him on an extremely long and dangerous journey to the Indian towns several hundred miles inland. They went to make a very important peace treaty with the Indians. In his description of their journey the Ranger wrote of how the Indians provided them with deer, turkeys and buffaloes. It was July and they saw grapes and other wild fruits not yet ripe. They saw several herds of buffalo, sixty or more in a herd. When they came to the Indian town after a month's journey they were brought fowls, venison, pumpkins, potatoes and watermelons. They were brought tea or "black drink" made from the leaves of holly and served in conch shells.

The Ranger wrote that the Indians hunted deer, turkeys, geese, buffaloes, bears, panthers, wolves and "tygers," which Bartram described as yellow panthers. Stephens's journal tells in 1740 that a tyger attacked a man working in a field only a mile from Savannah. He was able to shoot the beast while his dog kept it at bay. It measured eight feet long including a two-foot tail.

Smaller animals used for food and furs were raccoons, minks, rabbits, opossums, otters, beavers and squirrels. The most dreaded snake was the rattlesnake. Alligators were very plentiful and large, sometimes reaching eighteen to twenty feet in length. They could also be dangerous.

There were many songbirds. Travelers mentioned most often the redbird or cardinal and the mockingbird. One beautiful bird, the Carolina parakeet, is now unfortunately extinct. There were plenty of ducks and geese. Trout, perch, bass, catfish, sturgeon and other fish were plentiful, as were oysters and shellfish. The Rangers, who patrolled in the scout boats, could easily live off the fish in the region.

The bountiful wild life of Georgia could have provided the settlers with ample food for many years. But corn and vegetables had to be planted and tended and that left little time for hunting and fishing. The Trustees were most anxious to have each colonist plant a crop not only for the food it yielded but for produce that could be sent to England for sale there. They wanted to promote the growth of grapes and mulberry trees for making wine and silk. Some Trustees and scientists in England thought that tropical herbs, medicinal plants and tropical fruits could grow in Georgia.

Because of all these interests the Trustees made plans for a public garden to be planted and tended at Savannah. Before the first colonists sailed, the Trustees had appointed a botanist to travel to Madeira and the West Indies to gather plants and seeds for the garden. The first man, Dr. William

Houstoun, gathered some plants but he died in Jamaica in 1732. The next botanist appointed was Robert Millar, who also gathered plants for the garden in the West Indies.

A temporary nursery was set up at Charleston and the plants were sent there. It was under the direction of Paul Amatis, the Italian silk expert sent over on the *Ann*. The Trustees' or Public Garden in Savannah was laid out during the early days of the colony and put under the care of Joseph Fitzwalter while Amatis was in Charleston. Fitzwalter proved to be an enthusiastic gardener and wrote to the Trustees about his young plants. He spoke of orange trees six feet high that were expected to bear fruit that year. He had eight thousand mulberry plants for the silkworms. The olive trees had grown. He had planted cotton seeds from Guinea and had a thousand plants.

The kitchen garden area was Fitzwalter's special pleasure. In it he had grown wheat, barley, rye, oats, beans, peas, rye grass, clover and alfalfa seeds. There was rice and good Indian corn in plenty. Hemp and flax would do well. Fitzwalter liked to give away the garden bounty and thought that was its purpose. Oglethorpe appointed young John Goddard as his apprentice in the garden.

Francis Moore reported in his account that the garden was laid out to the east on a delightful setting along the Savannah River. Half the garden was on a hill, the rest on the side and at the foot of the hill. In the northern part there was a grove left over from the original woods, and it included the beautiful magnolia with fragrant blooms eight inches in diameter. The crosswalks were planted with orange trees. In the squares were planted quantities of mulberry trees for the silkworms. There were fruit trees such as apples, pears and peaches. There were olives, figs, vines and pomegranates such as grew in warm climates. There were tropical plants including coffee, coconuts, cotton, bamboo and tea. The garden was fenced and furnished with gates. We can imagine that when flourishing it was a favorite viewing spot for the colonists.

After such a good beginning rivalry between the gardeners led to eventual abandonment of the Trustees' Garden. When Paul Amatis came from Charleston he and Fitzwalter could not get along together. They could not agree how to plant or use the garden. Fitzwalter wrote he was once threatened by Amatis with a gun. Both quit the garden and the only other gardeners mentioned seemed much less interested in it and soon left. Heavy frost and drought killed many of the delicate plants. The garden required much care and the Trustees' servants made poor gardeners. Some of the discontent among the settlers in Savannah focused on the garden as a useless effort and expense.

William Stephens continued to mention it in his journal but mostly as a nursery for mulberry plants. He commented once that it took more trouble than it deserved and that the soil was poor. When William de Brahm, who became the king's surveyor, first came to Savannah in 1751 he found only two large olive trees and a few fruit trees left from all the experiments and work of the garden.

In 1755 Governor John Reynolds asked for a personal grant of the ten acres formerly known as the Trustees' Garden. It was made a residential area and houses were built on it. The area continued to be called the Trustees' Garden and is still called so today.

Indian Friends 5

The colony of Georgia was most fortunate in keeping the friendship of its Indian neighbors. In spite of wars with Spain and France during the colonial period, the Georgia Indians never deserted their English friends. There was a bloody war between the Cherokees and the South Carolina colony in 1760 but Georgia was not involved. Fear and danger did haunt the colonists during periods when Indian loyalty seemed to be turning toward the French or Spanish. From time to time there were alarms and small raids which resulted in loss of property and even lives of colonists and Indians. But these troubles were never allowed by Indian leaders or colonial officials to break the peace which both groups wished to keep.

The Indians had not objected when Oglethorpe selected the site of Savannah. Although they had an earlier promise from the British in South Carolina that no white people would settle on the Georgia side of the Savannah River, Tomo-chi-chi, chief of the Yamacraw tribe who lived there, agreed to let Oglethorpe have land for the colony. He also agreed to persuade the other Indian tribes to give their consent.

At the time Georgia was settled there were powerful Indian tribes who lived in and claimed the territory covered by the Georgia charter. The Yamacraws were a small tribe thought to include both Creek and Yemassee Indians. Most of the other Indian tribes lived much farther inland though their hunting lands ranged to Georgia's coastal islands.

The two most important and largest tribes were the Creeks or Muscogees and the Cherokees. The Uchees, a smaller tribe, lived on the upper reaches of the Savannah River. The Cherokees lived in the hills and mountains to the north in what is now Georgia, Tennessee and North Carolina. South of them was the powerful Creek Confederacy. This confederacy included many tribes banded together for protection and waging war. There were the Upper Creeks and the Lower Creeks, which included among their members the Ocmulgees, Oconees, Coosas, Cowetas, Alibamons and Talapoosas.

Farther west nearer the Mississippi lived two more tribes: the Chickasaws, who remained friendly with the English and the more numerous Choctaws, who were mostly allied with the French. The Choctaws were called Flatheads because they bound their babies' heads to make them flat in back and front. All these tribes were continually making raids or sending small war parties against each other. War was the proud occupation of the Indian braves. During most of the colonial period the larger tribes greatly outnumbered the Georgia settlers, who were at times almost defenseless.

The Creek and Cherokee Indians were more settled than some American Indian tribes. They lived in permanent towns where they cleared fields and grew crops. But their hunters and warriors travelled hundreds of miles while the women, children and older men stayed home and tended crops. A diary of a Frenchman in 1741 tells of being cap-

The Creek tribe was one of the largest and most important of those in the Georgia area.

tured by Cherokees while on a boat trip on the Ohio River.

The houses of Indian towns were situated at some distance from each other because each home was surrounded by its own fields. The center of the town was the public square where all important events—meetings, feasts, and dances—took place. Around the square were the houses of the chief or mico, the war chief or head warrior, and the beloved man or older warrior and wise counselor.

There was a town house where meetings took place in winter or bad weather. It was also called the "hot house" and was used as a public sleeping place in cold weather because it was kept warm. Their buildings were constructed of wooden posts or poles plastered over with clay mixed with grass. The roof might be covered with cane, palmetto leaves, tree bark, moss or earth. Along the inside walls of the houses were raised platforms or couches. These were covered with skins or furs on which they sat and slept.

According to William Bartram these Indians were tall,

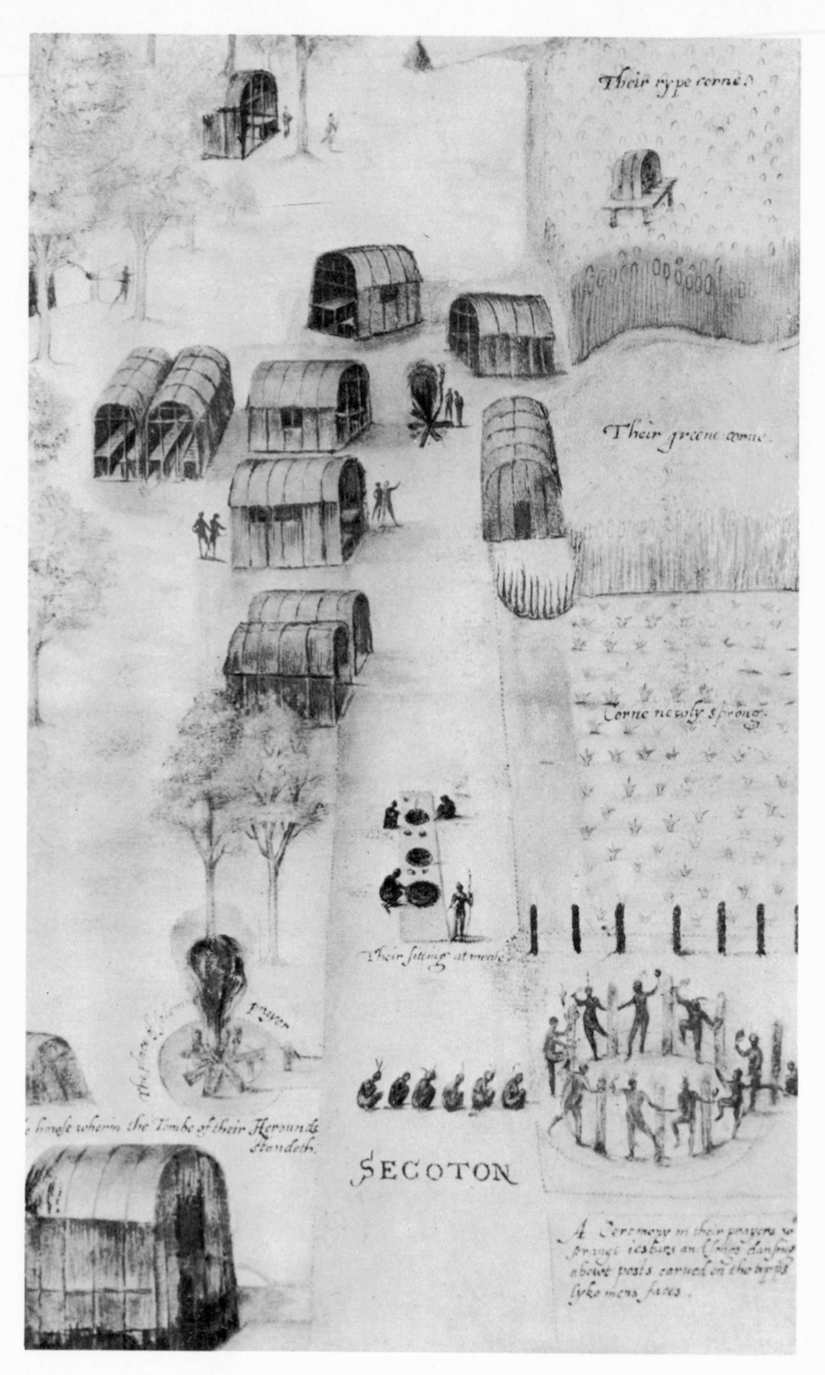

Corn was vital to the livelihood of the Indians.

erect and well shaped with regular features. They had reddish-brown or copper-colored skin and long black hair. They were graceful, dignified and independent. Oglethorpe further described them: "The men paint themselves red, blue, yellow and black. The men wear generally a girdle with a piece of cloth drawn through their legs and turned over the girdle front and back. The women wear a petticoat to the knees. In winter they wear mantles almost two yards square wrapped around their bodies leaving their arms bare. Their shoes are a kind of pump made of deer skin called a moccasin."

In another letter Oglethorpe wrote how the Indians lived: "They have plenty of Indian corn, pumpkins, potatoes, mush melons, water melons, peas, peaches, plums, nectarines and locust trees. They have fowls and hogs in abundance and some cows and horses. . . . They use the fat of the bear for oil and honey combs for sugar."

The forests furnished deer, turkeys, partridges and wild geese. There were plenty of fish and the Indians were expert fishermen. They ate wild fruits such as grapes and strawberries. They gathered hickory nuts and knew how to use wild roots and herbs.

The Indians were divided into clans or large families. Some clans were named for animals as the Bear, Beaver, Racoon, Eagle, Wolf, Deer, Alligator and Panther clans. They liked dancing, singing and playing games. There were war dances, festival dances and victory dances in which both the men and women participated. Their instruments were cane or bone flutes, rattles made from shells and drums. Their favorite games were chunkey, a game played with a round stone disk and a stick, and a ball game played on a field with opposing teams and two goals. The ball game was much like lacrosse with players using a racquet and a deerhide ball.

Their most important festival was the yearly busk, the

Tomo-chi-chi told Oglethorpe that the English were as swift as a bird and as strong as a beast.

celebration of the ripening of the main corn crop and of the beginning of a new year. It was a time of purification and rejoicing. The houses were swept clean and new pots replaced the old ones. The men drank a purifying black drink and bathed in the river. A new fire was kindled by friction and carried to all houses. The new corn was gathered and eaten and then there was general feasting and dancing. The busk lasted four or eight days. It was a new beginning and all crimes except murder were forgiven.

In the early days of the colony the Indians sent warriors on many occasions to help the English settlers against the Spaniards who were their enemies also. They were eager to have English goods such as guns, powder and cloth in exchange for their deerskins. Some chiefs, like Tomo-chi-chi, wished to be allied to the English because they felt the Indians could learn from them.

Tomo-chi-chi once gave Oglethorpe a buffalo skin painted on the inside with the head and feathers of an eagle. He told Oglethorpe the English were swift as a bird and strong as the beast and could fly over the water. The feathers were soft and signified love and the buffalo skin was warm and meant protection. Thus he hoped the English would love and protect the Indians' families.

The old mico was from the beginning a true and noble friend to the colonists. He was a very close friend of James Oglethorpe. It was his influence that brought the Creek chiefs to Savannah to make a treaty of friendship with Georgia. Tomo-chi-chi gave valuable advice to Oglethorpe and furnished trusted guides. He and other friendly chiefs provided warriors and went on military expeditions with Oglethorpe. When Oglethorpe returned to England for a visit in 1734 he invited Tomo-chi-chi and some other Indians to accompany him. The old mico, his wife, Scenawki, his great-nephew Toonahowie, six Indian chiefs and their attendants visited England. They met the King and Queen and spent time with Oglethorpe at his home at Godalming. They were a great success in London and returned home four months later with many presents including a gold watch from the Duke of Cumberland for Toonahowie, Tomo-chi-chi's nephew.

When Tomo-chi-chi died in 1739 he was probably nearly a hundred years old. He asked to be buried in Savannah near his friends the English. He was buried with full military honors in Percival Square, now Wright Square, in Savannah, where his monument can be seen. His nephew Toonahowie fought against the Spaniards at Frederica and was later killed fighting the Spaniards near St. Augustine.

Mary Musgrove, whose Indian name was Cousaponakeesa,

was also very important to the early Georgians. Her father was an English trader and she went to school in South Carolina. Her mother was the sister of "Emperor" Brim, a Creek chief, which gave her great influence with the Creeks. Oglethorpe met her when he first landed in Georgia and soon she began acting as interpreter.

Mary and her husband John Musgrove had a trading house on the Savannah River near the new town. Many Indians and colonists, including John Wesley, visited the house for Mary was a good hostess. Oglethorpe continued to call on her for help as interpreter. At his request she even moved her trading house one hundred and fifty miles inland on the Altamaha River and called it Mount Venture. Oglethorpe wanted her to be in the middle of Indian country and nearer the Spaniards. There she could watch the Spaniards and influence the Indians to be friendly.

When requested by Oglethorpe, Mary would go on trips to act as interpreter. Her first husband, John, died and she married Jacob Matthews. When he also died she married Thomas Bosomworth. While Oglethorpe was in Georgia, Mary remained a good friend. When he left Georgia he gave her a diamond ring from his own finger in friendship and gratitude. After Oglethorpe left and under the influence of her third husband, Mary's attitude began to change. She felt she had not been paid what was promised her; with no powerful person like Oglethorpe to take notice of her, she felt unappreciated. What happened when Mary turned against Georgia is an exciting story for another chapter.

The settlers made several important treaties with the Indians, who continued to cede land to Georgia. All the officials in Georgia from Oglethorpe's time to the royal governors understood the importance of the Indians' friendship and tried to be fair in their dealings with them. When the Indians visited the Georgia officials they were welcomed with gifts and entertainments. When the Creeks, Cherokees,

Choctaws and Chickasaws called an important meeting at Augusta in 1763, it was attended by seven hundred Indians and the governors from Virginia, North and South Carolina and Georgia.

It is good to remember the Indians' friendship in the early period. It was not until after the Revolution, when the Georgians demanded more and more land, that the Indians turned against them. Terrible deeds were committed by both sides before the Indians were driven out of Georgia. Georgians can be grateful for their friendship in the early days when a very weak frontier colony was almost surrounded by enemies.

The Indians have left us many beautiful and musical place names in Georgia. It is thought that the Savannah River takes its name from an Indian tribe of that name. Some authorities say it was called Sowanoka or Sauvannogee, a name for the Shawnee Indians who lived there at one time. It was called Sowanoka Hatchee meaning "river of the glades." One should remember that the Indians had no written language and names were written down as they sounded to the white man.

Spanish Foes 6

In the early years of the colony, Georgia needed her Indian friends. The Spaniards in neighboring Florida were not only unfriendly; they actually claimed the Georgians were trespassing on Spanish territory. Both Spain and England had claimed that section of the Atlantic coast and the dispute had not been resolved by the time Savannah was settled. Spanish threats and alarms and raids by Indians allied to Spain continued to harass Georgia for nearly half its colonial period until a final agreement was reached.

Spain had built forts and missions in what is now Georgia and Florida as early as the sixteenth century. Before this De Soto and other Spaniards had explored parts of Georgia. The Spanish called the province Guale (pronounced Wallie), after an important Indian chief of the area. A Georgia scholar relates how the Spanish explorer Menendez landed on St. Catherine's Island in 1566 and made friends with the Indian chief Guale. They sat together on the beach and ate biscuits and honey. When Charleston was settled in 1670 there were Spaniards living in the area that was to become Georgia.

The main interest of the Spanish was to increase their wealth and influence in the New World by establishing colonies. Their second aim was to convert the native Indians to Christianity. During this period Jesuit and Franciscan missionaries were sent to teach and baptize the Indians. There were Spanish forts and missions on the Georgia coast, particularly on the islands of Cumberland, St. Simon's, Sapelo and St. Catherine's. There were also some missions in southwestern Georgia. Not only were there soldiers and missionaries but Spanish farmers were sent to till the land and grow food for the soldiers. It is likely that some fruits like oranges and peaches found growing in Georgia by the British settlers were introduced by the Spanish. Spanish soldiers went as far inland as the Chattahoochee River in search of gold and established a fort, probably near present-day Rome.

The Spanish missions had their troubles. There were Indian uprisings and pirate raids which brought massacres, lootings and burnings. Sometimes Spain failed to send food, arms or supplies. The English colony established in Jamestown in 1607 was cause for alarm and increased Spanish interest in Guale. When Charleston was founded in 1670 there were said to be thirty-five Spanish missions scattered over Florida and Georgia. Spain greatly resented the new Carolina colony, and trouble between them began almost at once. Each attempted to drive the other out and encouraged the Indians to turn against its rival. Finally about 1702 the Spanish withdrew to St. Augustine, leaving the Georgia coast free of Spanish settlements.

The Spanish had not given up their claim and they strengthened their forces on the Gulf Coast and inland. The French also had a strong foothold on this coast and on the Mississippi. Spain, France and England continued their rivalry for this southeastern area, especially for the Indian trade. As a result of these unsettled conditions, in 1721 Carolina built Fort King George on the mouth of the Altamaha River near a Spanish mission site. The soldiers hated the conditions there and found the climate unhealthy. It was abandoned in a few years.

When Oglethorpe brought the first colonists to Savannah, neither England nor Spain had a settlement in this disputed territory. Spain naturally resented the Georgia colony and, according to Oglethorpe, Spain's spies were active from the beginning. The threat from Spain made Oglethorpe realize that the Georgia colonists needed stronger military protection in the south. Accompanied by Rangers and two Indian guides, he explored the coast south of Savannah and picked St. Simon's Island as the site of a new town and fort.

On his first return to England in 1734, Oglethorpe was able to convince the Trustees and Parliament that a new military settlement was needed. A company of brave and sturdy Highlanders from Scotland were recruited to come with their families to live in Georgia at Darien, on the mouth of the Altamaha. The Trustees also selected a large new group of colonists for St. Simon's, with Francis Moore as storekeeper. The ships bearing Oglethorpe, colonists, supplies and arms arrived at Tybee Island early in 1736. From there some went to the mainland while others set off south in periaguas to St. Simon's Island to found the new town of Frederica. If one of the big, flat-bottomed periaguas trailed behind, Oglethorpe's boat would tow it. On arrival Oglethorpe laid out the town and fort, and work began at once. Ten miles away on the mainland the industrious Scots Highlanders had made progress on their new settlement at Darien.

The colonists found St. Simon's an island with thick woods, marshes and a pleasant climate. There were many huge oak trees from which hung long garlands of Spanish moss. They found some cleared land where Indians had formerly grown crops. A colonist from Brazil taught them to build bowers covered with large palmetto leaves. Each family lived in a bower on their own lot until houses were built. Francis Moore, the storekeeper, wrote that these bowers "twenty feet long and fourteen feet wide . . . looked very pretty." The colonists planted orange trees on their twenty-five-yard-wide streets.

Frederica and its fort were built on the elbow of a river to control the approaches in both directions. On the southern tip of St. Simon's a fort was built to command the sea approaches. Oglethorpe ordered a road cut through the thick woods to connect Frederica with the fort some miles away. This road proved an important defense against the Spanish. As the settlers began to clear and cultivate the land Frederica grew into a flourishing town.

Oglethorpe set up forts on several islands south of St. Simon's. The friendly Indians were helpful and enthusiastic. The Spanish were suspicious and protested to England and to Oglethorpe. Meetings and agreements between the Spaniards and the English kept an uneasy peace. Oglethorpe had difficulty restraining the Creeks from attacking the Spaniards and their Indian allies. Spies were busy and rumors of a Spanish attack spread in the Georgia settlements and in Carolina. The colonists practiced military drill and target shooting. The English forts and Oglethorpe's bold military actions were not legal in Spain's eyes. The situation between the two nations became worse as Spanish ships stopped and searched British trade ships smuggling in Spanish waters.

When Oglethorpe again went to England in 1737 to seek military aid for Georgia, he managed to convince Parliament that the colony was in danger. He was given funds and permission to raise a regiment of soldiers. They made him commander in chief of all British forces in South Carolina and Georgia. The next year Oglethorpe returned to Geor-

Jenkins created a stir in Parliament over the outrage which led to the Battle of Jenkins' Ear.

gia with six hundred soldiers, most of whom were stationed at the forts on St. Simon's. Many brought their families and built homes on the land they were given for raising crops. These soldiers were described as having a hoe in one hand and a sword in the other. Frederica prospered even more and became a lively social town.

War between England and Spain broke out officially in 1739. The war was concerned more with sea power and trade than with land disputes and was fought mainly in the Caribbean Sea and in Georgia and Florida. It was called the War of Jenkins' Ear. This strange name came from an incident involving Robert Jenkins, who was master of a ship seized by the Spanish for smuggling in disputed Florida waters. According to Jenkins the Spanish cut off one of his ears as punishment before they released him. Whether the story was true or not, it eventually created a stir in Parliament. The British people were enraged by this example of Spanish arrogance and demanded war with Spain.

Oglethorpe prepared at once to take the offensive. He called for his Indian allies, collected his regular troops and recruited from the Georgia colonists. The response from the colonists must have been good. William Stephens, the Trustee's secretary, often mentions in his journal how few men were left in Savannah because most were away defending the colony.

By 1740 Oglethorpe was ready to attack the Spanish with two thousand troops, more than half of whom were Indians from friendly tribes. Marching south, this army captured several Spanish forts and laid siege to St. Augustine. The siege had to be abandoned, however, because the English fleet was unable to give enough support and the troops were weakened by recurrent outbreaks of fever. According to most accounts the South Carolina troops gave only half-hearted help. Both sides retired to prepare for further military actions.

During the war with Spain, Frederica became the center of Georgia's activities. Oglethorpe was the unofficial head of the colony and made his headquarters there. The war had its effect on all Georgia settlements but in different ways. Savannah suffered from a population drain. Some families fled in terror of the Spaniards and Indians. In the most dangerous periods the women and children had to be moved to a safer place like Ebenezer, the Salzburger settlement. A guard had to be on duty at all times of the day and night, both in the town and on the coast at Tybee to look out for invasion ships. The men who remained were the town's only defense and they had to be mustered, drilled and armed. William Stephens tells of the men being mustered by the beat of drums. The number of defenders against a Spanish invasion seems very small. At one time Stephens mentions 130 who answered the call to arms. Another time he speaks of only 70 able men "besides a party of youngsters, who would not easily rest contented to be beaten, or run away to avoid it."

One of the Georgians' worst problems was being cut off from news and supplies. The Spanish ships captured many vessels going to and from England and trading ships supplying the Atlantic coast. Supplies and money were often dangerously low. Lack of news and direction from England was very disheartening. All the coastal settlements were subject to Spanish raiding ships and inland Georgians were threatened by raids from Spain's Indian allies. Alarms and lack of manpower cut down on the amount of food crops. Trade languished. This state of affairs continued off and on for some years until peace was finally made with Spain. Except for skirmishes at the frontier forts, St. Simon's was the only place actually invaded by the Spanish.

Oglethorpe's expedition laid siege to St. Augustine.

In the spring of 1742 the Georgians knew that a big Spanish invasion was being planned to destroy the whole colony. By then England had troubles in Europe and could not send troops. South Carolina and the other American colonies did not respond to requests for military aid. Oglethorpe could count only on his own regiment and Rangers, besides Georgia volunteers and Indian allies. His forces numbered about nine hundred men, not all seasoned soldiers. Tomo-chi-chi's nephew, Toonahowie, now a young warrior, led a group of Indian braves.

Early in the summer of 1742 a Spanish invasion fleet of fifty-one ships sailed from Havana and St. Augustine with around three thousand men. Spanish documents show they had orders to destroy the settlements in Georgia and Carolina and lay waste to the plantations. Frederica was the first target.

Oglethorpe was a courageous and clever military leader. He believed his men, though greatly outnumbered, could more than match the Spanish and told them so. He prepared the people and defenses and set up lookouts. When word came that fourteen of the Spanish ships had gone to attack the two forts on Cumberland Island, Oglethorpe set out with three boats to go to its aid. There were fifty men in each boat. Under heavy fire from the Spanish, two of the boats managed to get through to the fort. The other boat came back and reported Oglethorpe was lost. When he returned the Frederica soldiers fired every gun in the harbor for joy.

The main Spanish fleet soon appeared off St. Simon's. The defenders at the sea fort had only the help of small boats and three ships. The largest of the three was the armed merchant vessel *Success,* loaned and commanded by Captain Thomson. All the defenders at the sea fort fought valiantly but could hold off the Spanish fleet for only a few hours. That night the *Success* and another ship escaped

Under heavy Spanish fire, Oglethorpe and his men scored a victory.

to Charleston to ask for help. Oglethorpe abandoned the sea fort after removing supplies and spiking the guns. The British withdrew to the town and fort of Frederica. There was no way to stop the Spaniards from landing near the abandoned sea fort and occupying it.

An escaped prisoner reported that the Governor of St. Augustine had accompanied the Spanish troops and that among the invaders were dragoons, grenadiers and a regiment of Negro soldiers with "Negro officers dressed in gold and silver laced clothes." At Oglethorpe's request a band of Indians remained in the woods and harassed the Spanish-occupied fort. Meanwhile Oglethorpe readied Frederica and its fort and offered to send off the women. Most of them would not go and remained "in good heart." He armed the servants and posted lookouts to watch for the enemy.

Very early a day later some two hundred Spanish soldiers marched toward Frederica, evidently the beginning of a major attack. Oglethorpe with the Highland company and the Indians rushed to meet them, followed by the Rangers and part of the regiment. It was a British victory. Oglethorpe himself captured two prisoners. Toonahowie was shot in the arm by a Spanish captain but saved himself by shooting the captain with a left-handed pistol draw. Fearing a Spanish attack on Frederica from the water, Oglethorpe left a detachment behind to guard the road while he returned with the remainder of the soldiers to Frederica.

A Spanish Grenadier captain with three hundred men reached this rear guard about three o'clock that rainy afternoon. There was a skirmish and in the confusion of smoke and rain the British began to retreat. When they reached a curve in the road Lieutenants Sutherland and Mackay decided to stop. Sutherland's platoon, Mackay's Highlanders and some Indians hid in ambush in the thick woods. When the Spanish troops reached that spot they stopped, assuming all the British had fled. The hidden soldiers must have watched in amazement as the Spanish stacked their guns and started to prepare dinner. A Highlander signalled by raising his bonnet on a stick and the attack began. The Spanish were entirely defeated and most were killed. Those who survived fled into the woods and adjoining marsh. Because the marsh water ran with the blood of the wounded, this encounter became known as the Battle of Bloody Marsh. Disheartened by their defeat, the Spaniards withdrew to the abandoned fort.

Oglethorpe decided to make a surprise attack and brought

most of his troops near the occupied fort by night. However, his plan was foiled by one of his emergency recruits, a Frenchman, who deserted to the Spanish and fired his gun to warn them. Oglethorpe withdrew his troops to Frederica, realizing the enemy would learn all his true weaknesses. He decided to send the Frenchman a letter pretending this deserter was sent to the Spanish as a British spy. In the letter Oglethorpe offered him money and directed him to delay the Spanish until a large British fleet came to their aid. As part of the ruse, a Spanish prisoner was freed and paid to take the letter to the Frenchman. Just as he hoped, the Spanish prisoner took it straight to his commander.

What were the Spanish to believe? Was this Frenchman an ally or a British spy? The officers could not agree. As they were debating the question Spanish lookouts spotted a few British ships coming from the north. These ships were on reconnaissance only and sailed back to Charleston when they saw the Spanish fleet. But the appearance of the ships convinced the Spaniards that the British fleet was on the way. They withdrew as fast as they could, "so downhearted they would hardly speak a word when they came on board" their ships. The Spanish sailed south and Frederica was saved.

It was a remarkable and providential delivery. Georgia had stood alone without help from England or its sister colonies. There was little that could have stopped the Spanish drive northward for Georgia's strength was at Frederica. Plantations were deserted and Charleston was reported "struck with panic fear." A Spanish victory would no doubt have changed American history. Spain would have regained the territory it claimed and Georgia again would have been Guale. Georgia continued to be harassed and threatened by Spain until Florida was ceded to England in 1763, but there was never again a real Spanish invasion.

A Miniature Melting Pot 7

The colony of Georgia had been planned by the Trustees as a haven for oppressed people from all over Europe. Therefore many colonists came whose native tongue was not English. Of course, from the beginning, interpreters were needed for the different Indian languages. Italians had come over on the first ship to teach the colonists silk culture. Soon people came to Georgia who spoke German, French, Scotch Gaelic, Irish Gaelic and Welsh Gaelic. Spain was considered an enemy but there must have been settlers who spoke Spanish. A variety of colonists made Georgia a place of many tongues, a polyglot colony. We call our United States a melting pot because of its many peoples. The youngest colony became a miniature melting pot as it absorbed the talents and characteristics of various peoples.

Georgia was growing. New villages, new towns, forts and settlements sprang up. In 1740 the Trustees demanded a report on the state of the colony. They wanted to know where the settlements were and how they progressed. It took a year or so to gather information from the scattered settlers. When the report was finished in 1741 there were about fourteen hundred inhabitants not counting the soldiers. Reading William Stephens's report is like taking a tour of early Georgia. Let's travel with him from Savannah, where there "are now 142 houses and good habitable huts. . . . Ships of about three hundred tons can come up to the town . . . and the river is navigable for large boats as far as the town of Augusta . . . 250 miles distant by water. There is already a considerable trade in the river. There is in this town [Savannah] a court-house, a gaol, a store-house, a large house for receiving the Indians, a wharf or bridge, a guard-house, and some other publick buildings; a publick garden of ten acres cleared, fenced and planted.

"Three miles up the river there is an Indian town," then considerable plantations and "at fifteen miles distance is a little village called Abercorn." Thirty-four miles up the river from Savannah is the "town of Ebenezer, which thrives very much; there are very good houses built for each of the ministers, and an orphan house. . . . They have partly framed houses, and partly huts, neatly built and formed into streets." Farther upstream there are Indian settlements, the Uchee Indian town and settlements on the Carolina side.

"On the Georgia side lies the town of Augusta, just below the falls. This was laid out by the Trustees' orders in the year 1735, which has thriven prodigiously. There are several warehouses thoroughly furnished with goods for the Indian trade and five large boats belonging to the different inhabitants." The report stated that these boats carried nine or ten thousand pounds of deer skins each and made four or five trips a year to Charlestown for export. "Hither all the English traders, with their servants, resort in the spring." Six hundred men and two thousand horses were estimated to be engaged in the very profitable Indian trade. The Indians brought their furs to trade for mostly "woolen and iron."

"At Augusta there is a handsome fort, where there is a small garrison of soldiers." Augusta was a valuable town because of its nearness to the Indians and the safety of the fort in case of troubles. The land around Augusta was fertile for farming. A road had been cut through the woods all the way from the Cherokee country through Augusta to Savannah.

Back at Savannah we begin another tour south down the seacoast. About five miles south and about a mile apart were the villages of Hampstead and Highgate and various plantations. Continuing south, miles and miles of wild coast and islands separated these villages from Darien at the mouth of the Altamaha River, "where the Scots Highlanders are settled. The buildings are mostly huts but tight and warm and they have a little fort. They have been industrious in planting and have got into driving of cattle. . . .

"Below is the town of Frederica, where there is a strong fort, and store houses, many good buildings in the town, some of which are brick. . . . There are some little villages on the Island of St. Simon's and some very handsome houses built by the officers of the regiment." Farthest south were Fort St. Andrew and Fort William on Cumberland Island. In the words of the 1741 report, "We are now fully acquainted with the colony."

The Trustees gave up their charter after twenty years and Georgia got its first royal governor in 1754, but the colony grew slowly until after the French and Indian War was over in 1763. People did not move into Georgia from other colonies until the restrictions on land, trade and slaves were removed. Georgia's exposed position in wars with Spain and France offered little safety to outlying settlers. When John Reynolds, the first governor, took office, he reported that Savannah contained only "about a hundred and fifty houses, all wooden ones, very small and mostly old." The governor reported that he used the biggest house for royal council meetings "but one end fell down whilst we were all there." The council had to move to a shed behind the court house temporarily. But after the war, conditions improved and new towns sprang up throughout the colony.

William De Brahm, in his history of Georgia, mentions the towns of Hardwick on the Ogeechee River, Sunbury on the Midway River, Wrightsboro on Little River and Queensboro upstream on the Ogeechee. These towns no longer exist. Savannah had two more suburbs, Acton and Vernonburg. People began settling the outlying lands, and the up country filled with people living on farms. The coastal plantations tended to be much larger in size than the upland farms. A few years before the Revolution, James Habersham wrote of the great increase of people in the back country, most of whom came from other colonies. These people had few or no slaves and were "ten fold the number on the same compass of land than they are on the sea coast." It is estimated that the population was about five thousand when Georgia became a royal colony and fifty thousnd when it became a state.

The town of Ebenezer was settled in 1734 by German-speaking people from a mountain valley of Salzburg. They were driven from their homeland because of their religion. The Roman Catholic Archbishop of that district told all Protestants they must leave. Thousands were exiled, some going to other parts of Germany, some to Holland, others to England. The Trustees of Georgia offered to send fifty families of exiled Salzburgers to Georgia. The first group was from Berchtesgaden and set out on foot from their home in the Alps to the port of Rotterdam. It was a very hard journey and they had lost all their possessions. But they frequently sang hymns. One stanza of their exile hymn can speak for all the many people who came to America for religious freedom:

My God conduct me to a place
  Though in some distant nation
Where I may have thy glorious word
  And learn thy great salvation.

When the Salzburgers reached Savannah they were thankful and joyful. They were welcomed by firing of cannon and hurrahs from all the colonists gathered on the riverside. The people served them food, and tents were erected for them on the town squares until their land was ready. Oglethorpe helped them select their land some miles upstream on the Savannah River. They went immediately to work.

Many of them had raised cows and sheep at home and had been miners and clockmakers and toymakers. But they knew something about farming. The Salzburgers proved to be orderly, hard-working, sober and pious people. Other Salzburgers came later. By 1741 there were said to be over a thousand German-speaking people in Georgia. This was probably more than the number of those who spoke English. Georgia's first Revolutionary governor, John Adam Treutlen, went to school at Ebenezer. The name Ebenezer is from the Bible and means "stone of help."

Another German-speaking Protestant religious group who came to Georgia in 1735 were the Moravians from Bohemia. They came primarily as missionaries to the Indians. They were granted land and were quiet, hardworking people.

A second group of Moravians arrived in Georgia early in 1736. They had sailed on the same ship with John and Charles Wesley and their friends Benjamin Ingham and Charles Delamotte. John Wesley served as Church of England minister in Savannah. He was much influenced by the Moravians' deep faith. The Moravians, aided by John Wesley and Charles Ingham, founded an Indian school near Savannah at New Yamacraw, Tomo-chi-chi's village. They had strict rules of living, with daily prayers and religious services. Their religion forbade them to carry arms or to fight. Their fellow colonists in Savannah came to resent this. During the worst of the threat from the Spanish, this resentment grew so much that the Moravians decided to leave Georgia. Many went to Pennsylvania.

Servants came over to help in the new colony. They agreed to work for a certain number of years to pay for their passage and supplies. Many Dutch and German people came to Georgia as indentured servants. Some English, Irish, Scottish and Welsh servants also came. When their work term was over they were granted land. The villages of Acton and Vernonburg were settled by these people. William Stephens often praised their industry and progress. Hampstead, one of Savannah's garden villages, was also settled by Germans. Highgate, another garden village, was settled by French-speaking families. Many of the Swiss people spoke French. A French-speaking minister came to Savannah for church services from the Swiss colony of Purrysburg in South Carolina.

A group of English-speaking Quakers came to Georgia around 1768 and settled the town of Wrightsboro on Little River in the Augusta area. They came from North Carolina. Joseph Maddock, one of their leaders, was visited by William Bartram while he was in Georgia. The Quakers named their town after the royal governor of Georgia, James Wright. The town and surrounding countryside granted to the Quakers probably had around two hundred families. They were a thrifty people and did not believe in slavery. Bartram reported a prosperous little village in 1773 with about twenty good houses. He bought cheese, butter, hominy and beef. Many Quakers moved away and Wrightsboro no longer exists.

One of Georgia's most thriving colonial ports, Sunbury, has faded into history. Sunbury, on the Midway River, was laid out in 1758 in the Midway district. It was settled primarily by the people from the Midway congregation, a Congregationalist group, originally from Massachusetts by way of South Carolina. They began moving to Georgia around 1752 and settled with their slaves in a swampy area to grow rice. Later the town of Sunbury was laid out on the Midway River between Savannah and Darien. In 1763 Governor Wright described Sunbury as a "well-settled place, having an exceeding good harbor and inlet from the sea. . . . There are eighty dwelling houses in the place, three considerable merchant stores for supplying the town and planters in the neighborhood."

As a port Sunbury began to rival Savannah. As many as seven large vessels would enter the port in one day. Indigo and rice were the principal crops. William Bartram also visited Sunbury and Midway meeting house about nine miles away. By the time of the Revolution much of the wealth of the province was in this district. It furnished many leaders of the Revolution and two signers of the Declaration of Independence, Lyman Hall and Button Gwinnett. Because of this, the area was given the name of Liberty County.

We have already mentioned the brave Scots Highlanders at Darien. Their community was spoken of as "one of the settlements where the people have been most industrious as those at Savannah have been most idle." They were Presbyterians and had their own minister, Mr. McLeod. Lt. Hugh Mackay was highly commended by Oglethorpe for his service in leading the settlers to Darien and commanding and building two forts. Lieutenant Mackay received one hundred pounds sterling from the Trustees for extraordinary services. He was praised as exhibiting that "public spirit which must be the support of all societies, and without which not only new colonies, but even the most powerful nations must perish." Some of the Highlanders spoke only Gaelic and wore their native tartans or plaids.

Hardwick and Queensboro, towns on the Ogeechee River, had a brief life. In 1755 Governor Reynolds decided to move the capital of the colony to the Ogeechee River to be nearer its center. He had a new town laid out to be called Hardwick. The plan to move the capital did not materalize

Oglethorpe visited the Highland colony and commended the settlers for their industriousness.

and Hardwick remained only a small trading village with the capital still at Savannah. Queensboro was settled by the Irish. It was about one hundred twenty miles upstream on the Ogeechee. About two hundred Irish families were said to live in the surrounding area but the town faded away. By 1771 a new town had been laid out on a coastal plantation near St. Simon's Island. It was named Brunswick.

In the first year of the colony, a shipload of Jews came to Savannah. They had not been sent by the Trustees but Oglethorpe accepted the new settlers, about forty in number. The first colonists had reason to be very grateful to one of them, Dr. Samuel Nunes, who arrived when many were deathly sick of summer fevers and other unknown complaints. Dr. Nunes treated them and was able to restore many of them to health. The colonists' own doctor had already died. The Salzburgers' minister, John Bolzius, makes mention in his journal of the kindness of the Jewish settlers. One of them gave all the newly arrived Salzburgers a meal of rice soup. Some of them, along with later Jewish settlers, became leading citizens of Savannah.

The slaves and the indentured servants made their own contribution to the colony with their labors. The African slaves added strange languages to those already spoken. The Trustees had reluctantly allowed slaves just before their charter ended. All the other colonies had slaves and it was very hard for Georgia to compete with them. There was just not enough manpower in Georgia of any sort. William De Brahm reported "scarce three dozen African servants" in 1751. By 1773 there were about fifteen thousand. Only about one-fourth of the people owned slaves.

The slaves probably came from the west coast of Africa, many from present-day Gambia. The European traders brought goods to Africa and the Africans exchanged slaves for these goods. Many slaves were captives of tribal wars.

But occasionally a greedy African chief would sell people from one of his own villages. Francis Moore thought that some African rulers had seriously weakened their kingdoms by selling their own subjects into slavery. Slaves were brought to the New World mainly by English, Portuguese, French and New England shipowners. There were also pirates who raided African villages and carried off slaves.

The terrible institution of slavery was accepted in most of the world at that time, though many people were against it. The American Indians owned slaves and frequently traded war captives as slaves. The Indian interpreter Mary Musgrove owned some Indian slaves. In very early colonial years the Indians traded or sold many Indian captives as slaves to the planters of the West Indies and South Carolina. The unlimited desire for European goods like iron, cloth, gunpowder and rum seemed to have a fatal effect on the American Indians and Africans. Some of them were determined to have these goods regardless of the cost to themselves or others. The white men had an insatiable desire for trade, land and cheap labor. Some of them were determined to have these things at any cost. Europeans, Americans, Africans and American Indians yielded to these desires and forgot their own humanity when they failed to respect that of others.

Many Georgia settlers had been victims of unjust actions or conditions. All over the world people have always been guilty of oppressing others and not accepting them as fellow human beings. To the Georgia colony came the poor and the unemployed, those persecuted for religion, the indentured servant and the slave in bondage. There were also many people looking for land and a new and better life. All these people of varied races, religions and languages made their contribution to Georgia. They made of Georgia a melting pot on a miniature scale.

Weekdays, Sundays and Everydays

8

A rugged pioneer of colonial Georgia could probably boast that he had slept on the ground, in a tent, in a rough lean-to made of branches, in an open boat and in an Indian lodge. He could also say he had slept in a log cabin, a hut, a modest town house and an elegant city mansion. Except for the Indians and traders, no person had built any shelters that the colonists could use. The colonists were free to follow their own plans and needs. As rapidly as they could, colonial Georgians built more comfortable houses for themselves.

Wood was in abundance and free so it was the natural choice of material. Building stone and clay for bricks was found close at hand. The stone was used for foundations. Frederica had brick houses before Savannah did. Bricks were brought from England in the early days to make chimneys. With the scarcity of labor, it was a long time before enough bricks were available. Some of the houses in Savannah even had wooden chimneys. These were such a fire hazard that a law was passed forbidding them.

An unusual material was used for building at Frederica and on the islands and coast. This was tabby or tappy. It was made of equal parts of lime, oyster shells and water and mixed into mortar. The mortar was poured into molds in a continuous row around the building and when the round or row had hardened, the mold was moved up to the next row. The outside had a stucco finish of lime and sand. The lime was made from the great quantities of oyster shells left by the Indians over the years. The fort at Frederica was a tabby fort as were some houses there. Many of the outlying forts, which had to be built quickly, were made of logs and earthwork.

The first frame houses at Savannah were all small and of uniform size, twenty-four feet by sixteen feet. They had sides of unplaned boards and shingled roofs. They were described as having one floor of three rooms and a cock loft with sleeping quarters. As the colony grew, finer homes were

Because wood was abundant, many colonists built log cabins.

As the colony grew, finer homes were built in the towns and on plantations.

built all over the colony in the towns and on the plantations. The more wealthy planter often had a town house also. One modest house had five rooms, four fireplaces, a front balcony, back piazza, dry cellars and garrets.

In 1764 a house on Bull Street in Savannah was advertised. It had two stories, a front balcony and a piazza. The first floor had a dining room, two bed chambers, two fireplaces, a passage and staircase. The second floor had a dining room, bed chamber, fire places and a closet big enough for a bed. There was a kitchen and paved cellar. Outhouses included a stable and chairhouse, for storing sedan chairs,

with two additional lodging rooms. Some houses contained rooms for shops or trades or professions. When they could, the colonists tended to build houses like those they left in Europe.

Public buildings were frequently made of wood with a brick or stone foundation. At first they were used for several purposes. The courthouse would be used for divine services and to entertain the Indians. Governor Reynolds and the council met in a large two-story house facing an open square. There was an eight-foot brick wall around it.

The colonists were anxious to have churches built but

it took them a long time to get enough money and materials. At first they worshipped in the shade of trees or in a tent. Then, while they were accumulating money to build proper churches, they used temporary structures or public buildings. When John Wesley arrived in Savannah in 1736, church services were being held in the court house and this practice continued for some years. The Savannah church was finally consecrated in 1744, but the building—of wood with a brick foundation—was not completed until 1750.

By 1740 both Ebenezer and Frederica had church buildings and by 1750 there were churches at Darien and Augusta. In most cases the Trustees and various church societies provided funds to build these early churches.

England wanted the colonies to produce food and raw materials, not to compete with English manufacturers. These aims are reflected in the range of occupations listed for the early Georgians who came from England. The most numerous occupations were servants, husbandmen, farmers, laborers, carpenters and weavers. The vine dressers, vintners and silkweavers in the colony also reflect the British desire for Georgia to produce silk and wine. Frontier life in Georgia compelled many of the colonists to change over to occupations suited to pioneering.

The wills left by Georgians during the colonial period reveal what their occupations were. The majority were planters but there were merchants and some Indian traders. There were mariners and shopkeepers, shoemakers, bricklayers and common laborers. There were vintners, saddlers, tailors, blacksmiths and gunsmiths. There were silversmiths, cabinetmakers and practitioners of physick (medicine). The Trustees encouraged pottery and potash making. Saw mills and grist mills were set up.

Supported by prosperity and aided by slave labor, coastal planters grew rice and indigo. Food crops, tobacco, and cotton were suitable for growth inland. It was some years before plows were used, and cultivating the land only with hoes must have been one reason for the colony's slow growth. All Georgians hunted and fished for food and recreation. There was lively traffic on the rivers and good shipping trade at Sunbury and Savannah. Much of Georgia's trade was with the West Indies.

In 1773 Governor Wright reported to England about the condition of trade. At that time Georgians owned five ships, one snow (a type of brig), seven brigantines, thirteen sloops and schooners, ten coasting vessels and river trading boats. He reported that 217 vessels had entered Georgian ports that year compared with only 45 in 1761. The main

Jerusalem church in Ebenezer, Georgia.

products in the trade were listed as rice, indigo, deer skins, raw silk, pitch, tar, turpentine, beef, pork, Indian corn, pease, tobacco, staves, shingles and lumber of all sorts. He also listed cattle, horses, beeswax and beaver skins.

The colonists were hindered by a lack of actual money. They could not make their own. A thousand pounds of silver coins and several tons of copper farthings and half-pence were sent from England. The Trustees used "sola bills" or bills of exchange. Spanish silver coins were used in Georgia along with English ones.

Colonial Georgia never produced much wine. The vines sent over were not suited to Georgia's climate. The most successful winemakers used Georgia's plentiful native wild grapes. Cattle raising was more widely practiced. The cattle herds were needed for food. Most of the colonists let their cows roam free in the woods. Large cowpens were located at various places to fence in the cattle when they were herded. Each cow was branded with the owner's mark. Cow-herds or cowboys rode on horseback to round up the cattle. There were rustlers too, who stole cattle and changed brands. These were serious offenses and rustlers were brought to justice. Many of these events were eighteenth-century cowboy dramas.

The darling dream of the Trustees and the crown was to outdo the European silk producers. Every encouragement was given Georgians to raise silkworms. Silkworm eggs were sent from Europe and were set out to hatch in the mulberry trees. But the industry seemed to flourish only when a bounty was paid for silk. First the Camuse family, then Pickering Robinson, then Joseph Ottolenghe were in charge of silk culture. Public filatures were built for silk reeling. In one of the biggest years, 1762, over fifteen thousand pounds of cocoons were raised and over a thousand pounds of raw silk were reeled.

In 1732 the *South Carolina Gazette* gave the following

account of silkworm raising. "It becomes a pretty big worm and shuts itself up in its cod or ball it weaves itself. This looks like a greenish bean. At length it becomes a butterfly after making its passage from its silken sepulchre." The idea was not to let the butterfly emerge from his cocoon. This would damage the six-mile-long silk thread it had spun. The account goes on to say that when ready the cods are "taken down and put in a moderate oven or exposed to the sun to kill the maggot. The cods are different colors, yellow, orange and flesh color. Some are green, some sulphur color, some white." By various means the silk is wound off and "the worm itself can be fed to poultry."

The worms did not take well to Georgia's variable spring climate. Labor was expensive and without a bounty the silk industry could not compete with other paying crops. The industry continued to exist but declined in interest and importance. By Revolutionary days very little silk was made. Georgia's best claim to silk fame was Queen Caroline's dress made of silk reeled in Georgia that she wore at the king's birthday celebration in London.

Some of the colonists must have worn silk for it was advertised by the merchants. After Georgia's early years, merchants began to import most goods and luxuries from England. Not all the colonists could afford them, however. A ledger of a Savannah merchant, Thomas Rasberry, lists a remarkable variety of merchandise ordered by him. There are all kinds and qualities of woolen, silk and linen cloth listed and all kinds of wearing apparel. On the list are leather gloves, painted hose, jewelry, fans and umbrellas. For some reason yellow was disliked and Rasberry asked that it not be sent. Items of most other colors were requested, including scarlet cloaks, red handkerchiefs and multicolored silk hats.

James Habersham, merchant and once acting governor, ordered a silk suit from England and mentioned his gay

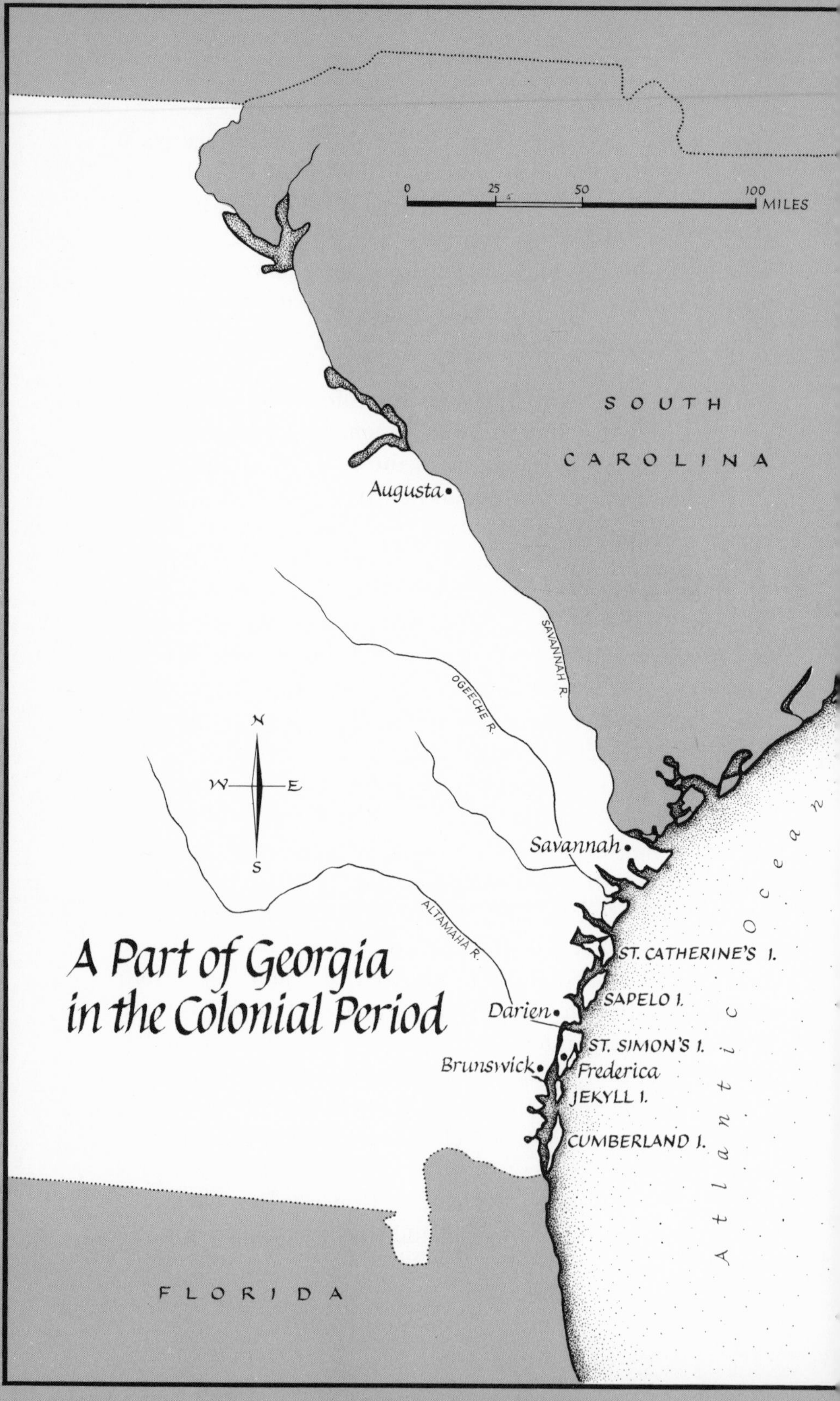

A Part of Georgia in the Colonial Period

0 25 50 100 MILES

SOUTH CAROLINA

Augusta

SAVANNAH R.

OGEECHE R.

N
W E
S

Savannah

ALTAMAHA R.

ST. CATHERINE'S I.

SAPELO I.

Darien

ST. SIMON'S I.

Brunswick

Frederica

JEKYLL I.

CUMBERLAND I.

Atlantic Ocean

FLORIDA

waistcoat. Oglethorpe ordered stroud (a coarse wool), thread and *osnaburg* for jackets and breeches for the scout-boatmen. The Scots at Darien wore their own colorful tartans. Cotton and linen were found to be most suitable for Georgia's summers. Any slave who showed courage in action while on military service received a reward. Each year he was given a livery coat and breeches of good red cloth turned up with blue, as well as a hat, shoes and stockings. He was given a holiday every year on the anniversary of his brave deeds. The Indians painted themselves and loved gaily colored beads and blankets. Colonial Georgia must have been a colorful place.

Court days in Georgia were busy ones. The jails were often very unsavory places, cold and dark. William Stephens called the jail the log house. Jails were poorly built and the inmates often escaped. Punishment was similar to that in England. There were fines and whippings. People were put in the pillory and the stocks and sometimes women were ducked. People could be put in jail for debt. Some of those convicted of murder were hanged.

News was hard to come by and depended on messengers by ship and horseback. Notices and news were often posted in a central place in the towns. The first newspaper, the *Georgia Gazette,* began in 1763. The editor, James Johnston, was also a bookseller. Among the books he advertised for sale were Swift's *Tale of a Tub* and *Gulliver's Travels, Robinson Crusoe, Aesop's Fables,* and works by Shakespeare. Also for sale were Bibles, Greek and Latin classics, poems, essays and religious works. Other merchants advertised children's primers and hornbooks, sheets of parchment with the alphabet and tables of numbers. Georgia had some libraries and there was a library society. In his history William De Brahm mentions three good libraries and stated that many families owned good books. Ministers and schoolmasters, of course, did too. Many books were donated by the Trustees.

Not everyone went to church on Sunday, even though churchgoing was encouraged. Thomas Jones complained of the noise of wheelbarrows rolling by the church door and the firing of hunting guns during church services. There were generally two services a day, one in the morning and one in the evening. At times the services were held in French, German and English. The members of other denominations also used the church house and on those days the church was never empty. The Church of England was the established church and members of other denominations were called dissenters. Dissenters in Georgia included Lutherans, Presbyterians, Quakers and Baptists. Many people lived far from any church and did not attend services unless a minister made a rare visit in their neighborhood. Ministers and teachers were scarce.

There were plenty of taverns and public houses to provide meeting places and entertainment. These houses served meals and some took in guests overnight. Beer was served as in England and later rum and other spirits when the Trustees' law against them was repealed. Public houses were licensed in Savannah, Ebenezer, Augusta, Sunbury and on the Northwest Road. At the London Coffee House in Savannah, dinner was on the table at half past one and beef steaks were served any time. Christian Etty's place, one mile west of Savannah, provided syllabub, a sweet dessert or beverage.

We have few records about what the women did for relaxation. If the women had time, they probably sewed and knitted and gossiped together in the towns and the wealthier hostesses served tea and coffee. On the lonely farms there was too much work to do and no companionship was at hand. Children had plenty of chores and older ones were apprentices. In their free time they swam in the rivers, despite the danger of alligators. All children would have envied those in Savannah. There Mr. Burquoin not only practiced "physick" or medicine but also sold white and brown sugar candy, Jordan almonds, barley sugar and raisins.

Daily chores of living kept all but the wealthy occupied. For women and children there was gardening, fetching wood and water, cooking, cleaning and washing. Cooking was generally done in the big kitchen fireplace and there was a public oven for baking bread. Iron pots and pans and iron and copper kettles were in use. Stoneware and earthenware, china, glassware, pewter and silverware were all on the family table. Merchants sold tin pots, pans, kettles and tin kitchens or ovens. The only light at night came from pine torches, oil lamps, lanterns or candles.

Daily life in Georgia was much like that of the other colonies in the eighteenth century. Town life was more varied, interesting, social and lively than country life. Each tradesman and artisan provided a different service. There were more things to buy. In the country people had to rely on themselves more and do without what was not available. They had to learn to do many things for themselves. The demands of frontier life thus encouraged the growth of the American spirit of independence.

From the colonial records we take the following description of Michael Burkhalter, cited as an exemplary planter: "an honest man and a regular liver, is master of several handycraft trades, such as a millwright, a wheelwright, a cooper and a carpenter. His eldest son is a shoemaker and carpenter; his son in law the same. His eldest daughter supplies the place of a taylor, and his five other younger children are daily trained in those trades. In all moderate weather they work in the lands, and when it becomes immoderate, or in the heat of the day, they come home and within doors work at their respective trades. Neither is this man less careful of observing the Lord's Day and performing continually religious duties in his family. And as he lives himself, so he brings up his children and his household in the fear of God."

Sinister Plots and Shining Days 9

For the children in colonial Georgia there must have been many shining and memorable days. There would have been the frequent Indian visits and encampments. Because of friendly relations, the colonists and Indians mingled freely. Often the Indians held festive bonfires and dancing which the colonists attended to their great entertainment. What a wonderful adventure to go out on the coastal creeks and rivers at night with the Indians! They fished with torches or built bright fires in the canoes and paddled over the feeding grounds. The fish, especially mullet, would be drawn to the light and jump in the boats. The expert Indians must have taught the older boys to stalk deer and bear.

Nature could provide wonder, food and fun. In the winter of 1743–44 appeared a comet visible for some weeks, "with a stream of light issuing from it almost upright . . . about two or three yards in appearance." There were the rare visits of great flocks of wild pigeons, filling the trees of the woods. They provided plentiful food to the taker "like quails to the Israelites in the wilderness." A natural and welcome job for the children was the gathering of wild berries, nuts and grapes in their season. Sometimes the all-night lime burnings on the coast were occasions of feast and frolic. There would have been the excitement of meeting a newly arrived ship from England or seeing a brave messenger galloping on horseback, both bringing news.

There were special days to celebrate or remember. For some years after the first time on board the *Ann*, Oglethorpe's birthday was celebrated. In 1737 the principal inhabitants met at the fort at noon and drank toasts to Oglethorpe, the Trustees, and the royal family, while thirteen guns were fired. In the evening there was a banquet and then a dance at one of the taverns. The king's birthday was celebrated with toasts and firing of guns. For a few years the anniversary of the founding of the colony was celebrated by firing of cannon. In 1740, Stephens hoped that "ages to come will celebrate this day annually here, in a better manner." According to Stephens, in 1739 the anniversary of the Freemasons was observed with a sermon, small parade and dinner.

Holy days and religious festivals were observed in colonial Georgia. The plan for the first church building had, on a very modest scale, been based on the Covent Garden Church in London. When the cornerstone was laid in 1744 there was a religious service with a sermon based on Psalm 122, followed by a small feast. St. Andrew's Day, November 30, was celebrated especially by the many Scottish people in the colony.

Christmas Day and Easter were observed by going to church. As in England, it was the two or three days after that were observed as holidays. At Christmastime the men would go hunting for wild turkey and other game for the holiday feasts. The main diversions were sports and games. Football, cricket and horse racing were favorite sports. Many were played in the town squares. The men practiced marksmanship. On the Easter holidays in 1741 a hat was

Growing wealth in the colonies was accompanied by increased interest in the arts.

given as a prize for the best shot. Raffles were held and once a horse, another time a canoe, were prizes.

The growing wealth of the colony brought more elegant entertainments to some. The large building no longer used as a public filature for silk reeling was let out for balls and other entertainments. The more wealthy could ride in coaches or sedan chairs. In 1766 the *Georgia Gazette* has this notice: "For the benefit of Mr. John Stevens Jr. on June 4th, the King's birthday, will be performed at Mr. Lyon's long room in Savannah a concert of musick. After the concert, musick will be provided for a ball. Tea, coffee, cards, etc. . . . Tickets for five shillings each." The royal governors added feasts and fire works to celebrations of the king's birthday.

Good relations with the Indians were of prime importance to all Georgians in colonial days. Governor Henry Ellis shines out as master diplomat in his relationship with the Indians. The Governor invited the Creek chiefs to

Savannah to gain their friendship in Georgia's struggle against Spain. In the fall of 1757 a large party of about one hundred and fifty Indians were camped on the Altamaha River on their way to Savannah. Governor Ellis sent Captain John Milledge and the Rangers at Ft. Argyle to conduct them to Savannah. Savannah made elaborate preparations to impress the visitors for the event was looked forward to as one of the most important Indian visits in colonial days.

When the Indians with Captain Milledge and the escort neared Savannah, they were met in a large field by the town leaders mounted on horseback. They were welcomed in the governor's name and feasted in a tent prepared there. Afterwards the company continued to Savannah led by the town personages on horseback with the Rangers as rear guard. When in sight of Savannah they were saluted by sixteen cannon. Inside the gate Colonel Noble Jones met them with the foot militia and conducted them to the Council Chamber.

As they passed Governor Ellis's house they were saluted with seven cannon from his battery plus those on the riverside and aboard the ships. They were met by a company of the Virginia Blues drawn up before the Council Chamber who saluted them with a volley of shots. The company formed two lines between which the Indians were conducted to the Council House. According to a contemporary account, they were "introduced to His Honour the Governor who holding out his hands addressed them in the following manner—'My friends and brothers, behold my hands and arms. Our common enemy the French have told you they are red to the elbows, view them, do they speak truth? Let your own eyes witness, you see they are white, and could you see my heart you would find it as pure, but very warm and true to you my friends.' " It was a most happy visit and the Indians were highly pleased to sign a treaty of friendship.

In 1744 nearly all of Savannah celebrated Mary Musgrove's third marriage, to Thomas Bosomworth. Thomas Bosomworth served for a short time as minister at Savannah until the Trustees removed him for neglecting his duties. The wedding celebration was held in the president's house (at first, Georgia's chief executives were called presidents, not governors) with great feasting and dancing. Little did those who honored this Creek woman and her husband dream that the couple would turn against them. In five years the Bosomworths brought about the greatest Indian danger Savannah had ever experienced.

Mary's service and support in the early years of the colony cannot be questioned. The prestige and influence which Oglethorpe had cultivated for her among the Creeks she later used to threaten the very existence of Georgia. This she did either under the direction of or in conspiracy with her husband, Thomas Bosomworth. The two of them managed to gain control over the powerful but unstable Lower Creek Chief Malatchee. Malatchee was described by another Creek chief as having a heart like the wind, or no heart at all. The Bosomworths waited until the regiment left Frederica, leaving Georgia very unprotected.

Thomas Bosomworth's scheme had been to persuade some Creek chiefs to declare Malatchee emperor of the Creeks. He then persuaded Malatchee to cede to the Bosomworths the three islands Ossabow, Sapelo and St. Catherine's. It appears the Bosomworths were land hungry and power mad. They wished to gain control over the Creeks as well as the presents sent them by the British government. They influenced Malatchee to declare Mary empress of the Creeks with full power over their actions.

Next, in the summer of 1749, the Bosomworths brought to Savannah about one hundred Creek chiefs and warriors —without the invitation of the town. They stayed almost a month and kept Savannah in a state of uneasiness and sometimes terror. Malatchee claimed that he was in Savannah to make certain Mary was not going to be sent to England in chains, as had been rumored. The other Indians probably came for entertainment and presents. The real issue was to see who exercised greater control over the Indians, the Bosomworths or the Georgia officials.

There were some very friendly meetings and dinners. There were also some very dangerous moments. The horse and foot militia were called and remained on constant duty. Captains Noble Jones and John Milledge and their troops showed themselves alert, brave and wise. One evening a party of Indians paraded by drumbeat around the town. At the same time a false report spread that the Indians had cut off President Stephens's head. The furious Savannahians armed themselves and were barely prevented from firing on the Indians.

At the many dinners given to entertain the Indians, Mary would sometimes rush in and furiously declare herself queen of the Creeks. Once in public she stamped her foot and declared all the land she stood on was hers. She also threatened to destroy Georgia. Everytime the Georgia officials had pacified the Indians, the Bosomworths would stir them up again. Another dangerous incident occurred at a dinner. Mary interrupted it and in a rage told Malatchee the Georgians were going to imprison her. He foamed at the mouth and ordered the Indians to arm themselves. They drew their tomahawks and only the quick command of Captain Jones and the guard that they lay down their arms prevented a disaster.

At the end of a long and frightening month, most of the Indians left. They had been pacified with presents and understood, besides, that the Bosomworths were only using them. Mary's claims were finally settled some years later when the British government granted her St. Catherine's Island, which was where she lived, and a sum of money.

Coosaponakeesa, queen of the Creeks, was once again plain Mrs. Bosomworth.

Oglethorpe and the Georgia officials complained during the Spanish period that Georgia was full of spies. We have records about two very colorful ones. John Savy of London was a real international spy whose story is told by Lord Percival, Earl of Egmont. Savy first settled in Charleston but went to Georgia to escape his debts. He sailed for London in 1735 but boarded a French fishing boat in the English Channel and went on to Paris, where he offered to give information about Georgia to the Spanish consular secretary there.

The Spanish government gave him money, passports, and a salary of one thousand pieces of eight a year. He became Captain Miguel Wall and told all. In Havana he had a change of heart when he heard of all the plotting against his country. He disguised himself and finally escaped to Lisbon. There he gave himself up to the British envoy and was sent to England as a prisoner in 1737. His testimony there helped convince the British to send troops to Georgia. Lord Percival said Savy made other confessions but no mention could be made of them "because they were matters that touched all Europe."

The character of the self-styled Jesuit Christian Priber remains a mystery. Some think he was a French spy. Others consider him a communist idealist whose aim was to set up his own dictatorship. He first appeared in 1736 among the Cherokees, living as one of them and speaking their language. They liked him and made him their official secretary. The English disliked his insulting letters and French leanings and the English traders disliked his teaching the Cherokees to use scales to weigh their furs.

The Cherokees protected Priber. He made a mistake when he went to spread his doctrine in the Creek country. There he was captured and taken by the British to prison in Frederica in 1743. Oglethorpe was astonished to learn that Priber spoke most European and American Indian languages fluently. He was very polite and spent his time in prison reading the classics. He had written a grammar of the Indian language.

Priber had with him a written description of the ideal state he wished to establish. It would welcome all fugitives and criminals, allow everyone to do as he pleased and be called Paradise. The gentlemen of Frederica were fascinated by him and visited him often. Before his fate was decided this idealist died in prison.

It is good to know that the colonists enjoyed some laughs in spite of their cares and dangers. All Savannah enjoyed the affair of the geese and the goats. Robert Williams let his goats run loose and Joseph Fitzwalter let his geese run loose. The goats feasted on everyone's garden, especially the prize garden of Joseph Fitzwalter, the public gardener. As the story goes, no fence could keep out the "cunning old he-goat." So Fitzwalter "slew the old leader." Williams swore revenge. He loaded his gun and stalked the streets of Savannah for geese. He fired at and scattered the first flock he saw which belonged not to Williams but to the widow Vanderplank. This "mad folly" provided the town weeks of merriment and the widow Vanderplank with an unexpected goose dinner.

Orphans and Apprentices– Pupils and Runaways

10

What did Georgia hold in store for the children? We met three London boys in the first chapter, Charles Clark, John Goddard and Marmaduke Cannon, who came with the first settlers. By 1734 all three were orphans with one or both parents dead. The hard life, strange fevers and the diseases of the frontier were the reason for so many orphans, rather than the wars. Some time later young Charles Clark also died, possibly of the common fever or flux. The record gives no details. There were trustees for the orphans who placed them in other families. Though John and Marmaduke inherited their fathers' lands, they had to work as all pioneers did.

We have already mentioned John Goddard as being apprenticed to Joseph Fitzwalter, the Trustees' Gardener. It would have been a good job to learn about all the exotic plants being introduced. There would be no danger of starving with a successful gardener like Fitzwalter. John did not remain a gardener's apprentice and later was a servant to Thomas Christie, who also came over on the *Ann*. John became a runaway apprentice and, according to William Stephens, was "mostly on the ramble" in 1743.

This is not hard to understand for a young man with no family ties. John sold his good town lot in Savannah, too cheaply, according to Stephens. He reported "this extravagant young man . . . in a few days had not a penny . . . left." Let's hope he enjoyed spending the money. Later he took a job on Noble Jones's guard boat at Skidaway Narrows.

The orphan Marmaduke Cannon went to live with the Trustees' storekeeper Thomas Causton. He worked on Causton's farm at Oxstead, a few miles from Savannah. Stephens saw him there in 1736, "a lively youth." By 1740 rumors were spread that Marmaduke was being mistreated. He was brought before the town officials to tell his own story. Stephens described him as a "tall lad; at least five feet high, and could hardly read his primer." Marmaduke was "in miserable rags, weeping."

Oglethorpe had ordered all freehold orphans (those who owned land) to learn to use a gun and stand guard duty and they "were delighted at it." Stephens told the boy that he did not want to lose a soldier. He said that Marmaduke must appear with his gun for guard duty that evening. What joy this manly duty must have brought a dejected boy. He did his night's duty and the next day decided to enter the Reverend George Whitefield's orphanage. Whitefield was a famous clergyman who had founded an orphanage. The next year Marmaduke was apprenticed to a Savannah carpenter. We can imagine that he manfully appeared with his gun whenever there was a call to arms during the Spanish threat.

The need for an orphanage must have been discussed by Oglethorpe and Charles Wesley, his secretary. Charles Wesley was at Frederica in 1736 for a brief stay. George Whitefield praised this "noble design in the General" and wrote that Charles Wesley passed on the idea to him. Another orphanage was already in existence in Georgia, which no doubt impressed Oglethorpe. The Salzburgers at Ebenezer made the care of orphans one of their first duties. They set aside a house for this purpose before a regular orphanage was built. It must have been the first Protestant orphanage in America.

The Salzburger ministers, Mr. Bolzius and Mr. Gronau, had both been at the famous Latin orphan house in Halle, Germany. The care of orphans was naturally one of their first thoughts. Money to help build the orphan house was sent from Europe. Work on the building began in 1737 for there were already many orphans. It was finished in 1738 and in three years all debts were paid. The orphanage was built before there was a church and church services were held there for four years.

This orphanage was a two-story building forty-five by thirty feet and twenty-two feet high. It was divided into three living rooms, three bedrooms, a roomy kitchen and pantry. At a distance were a cow stall, pig barn, chicken barn, bake oven and wash kettle. When it opened there were twelve orphans. There was a superintendent and a matron and probably some widows to help take care of the children. There was plenty of wholesome food and plenty of work to do.

The children got up at five o'clock, dressed and washed and met for morning worship led by a minister. Before breakfast the boys worked in the garden and the girls had household duties. After breakfast, they went to school until noon. We know they were given religious instruction and learned to read and write. We do not know if they all studied Latin, French, English, German and mathematics as Governor Treutlen did under Mr. Bolzius. Another teacher gave them English lessons. After the noon dinner, there was a break until four o'clock, then more duties. In the evening there was a prayer service and the children studied the catechism before bedtime.

Discipline was strict but there was time for play. The boys played and lived in the left side of the orphanage and the girls in the right. The orphanage was visited and praised by Oglethorpe, John Wesley, and George Whitefield. Oglethorpe gave the orphanage forty pounds and Whitefield gave some money and a church bell. The orphanage also took in widows and sick men if they accepted the rules. There were twenty-one people in 1738. The orphanage is little mentioned after 1750.

George Whitefield was an enthusiastic man and one of the greatest preachers of the eighteenth century. He came to Georgia as a minister of the Church of England but the orphanage idea took his whole attention. He went all over the American colonies and England collecting money for a Georgia orphanage to be called Bethesda, or "house of mercy" in Biblical Aramaic. Land was granted for it fifteen miles south of Savannah on the inland waterway across from Noble Jones's plantation.

Work on Bethesda began early in 1740. Business was very bad in Savannah that year. People were glad to work for pay at the orphan house. Whitefield would not wait for it to be finished. He rented a house in Savannah and began gathering orphans to add to some brought with him. He had brought a schoolmaster, James Habersham and a superintendent, the Reverend Charles Barber, from England. While the orphanage was in Savannah, it held a day school with Habersham as the teacher.

When finished, Bethesda was an impressive place. The main building consisted of two stories, sixty feet long and forty feet high. It was "a grand edifice," with twenty rooms. Within the great fenced garden were several other buildings. There was an infirmary, a workhouse for women and children, a kitchen, wash house, stable and storehouse. There was plenty of land for cultivation of food and crops. Stephens often wrote of the "orphan boat" which made regular trips to Charleston for supplies. Two schoolmasters and two schoolmistresses, a nurse, a tailor, a joiner, a weaver and a shoemaker became part of the Bethesda staff. When slavery was allowed, nearly fifty slaves were added to the Bethesda group. When there was time off from work, the slave children went to school.

When Marmaduke Cannon went to Bethesda there were children there with whom he had played aboard the *Ann*. The orphans must have greeted him with this song:

> Welcome dear Brother, whom we love
> Bethesda this we call
> A house of Mercy may it prove
> To you, to us, to all.

At Bethesda, Marmaduke was under a strict schedule. Up at five for prayers and religious talk. At six to church for psalms and a lesson. Breakfast at seven with prayers and assigning duties. From eight to ten, work at various duties as cleaning, woodcutting or helping the carpenter, tailor or shoemaker. The girls would sew, knit, card, spin or pick cotton and wool and some did household work. School was from ten to noon, then more work directly after dinner until two. More school from two to four, then back to work from four to six. After supper, church, and at eight all went home for religious examination. Then bed at nine after prayers. Mr. Whitefield allowed no idle hands for Satan to use at Bethesda.

It must have been a joyful break in a rigid routine when all the orphans fled to Port Royal from the Spaniards in 1742. Bethesda then took in refugees from Darien and parts south. It remained in continuous operation until a fire destroyed the buildings in 1772. It had cared for one hundred eighty-three orphans, including two blind boys and other poor and sick people.

George Whitefield died in 1770. He was greatly mourned

in the American colonies. The young Negro poetess, Phyllis Wheatley of Boston, wrote a memorial poem about him. Whitefield had already written his own funeral hymn which he had planned for the Bethesda orphans to sing. But because he died in New England the orphans were spared from singing the twelve doleful verses at the funeral.

Other Bethesda children besides Marmaduke appear in later Georgia history. Peter and Charles Tondee and Lachlan McIntosh lived at Bethesda for a while. They might have slept in one of the sleeping chambers furnished with four bedsteads and four feather beds. George Whitefield had two unwilling inmates at the orphanage. John Milledge was eleven when he came over on the *Ann* with younger brothers and sisters. After the death of John's parents, Oglethorpe helped John to go to England and there arrange to lease his father's Georgia land to provide for the family. John acted as its head and kept the children together. Oglethorpe helped them and gave John work. Although the Milledges were managing to get by, Whitefield took away young Frances and Richard from John and Sarah, the oldest sister. With the help of Oglethorpe the family was reunited. The Milledge children were probably the only orphans who ever bested the strong-minded Whitefield.

One of Georgia's first and most interesting schools was the Indian school called Irene. The Trustees had agreed to pay for the materials if the Moravian missionaries would build an Indian school, so the Moravians built a three-room schoolhouse near Tomo-chi-chi's village, New Yamacraw. At the school Ingham and the Moravian missionaries taught reading and writing to Indian children and any adults who wanted to come. They also taught them to sing hymns, which the children especially liked. However, the Spanish war loomed and the Indians went off to prepare for war. The Moravians had to leave and Irene was closed forever.

During the Trustee period there was a free school in Savannah. The first teacher was Charles Delamotte. He was so well liked the whole town went to the riverside to see him off when he left. No teacher stayed long and some were not very good. John Dobell was a teacher who was proud enough of his students to send samples of their writing to the Trustees. Sometimes the ministers served as teachers also.

There were private schools of various kinds in Georgia from time to time. They grew in number as the colony became more prosperous. James Seymour, who became a minister at Augusta, ran a school. Boarding schools opened, even some for girls. According to advertisements in the *Georgia Gazette* some of these schools offered classes in languages, mathematics, grammar, navigation, needlework, dancing and music.

Some Georgians were concerned over education for the slaves, who already suffered a language handicap. Bartholomew Zouberbuhler, rector of Christ Church, Savannah, left in his will over a thousand acres to be used to hire someone to teach the slaves Christianity. A condition was that any slave who became a competent teacher was allowed to teach other slaves. James Habersham helped carry out the terms of the grant in 1766. He made the teachers available to his own slaves and any other planter who desired them. Many of the slaves became very skilled artisans. Their work was hired out in the towns and some of them rented houses in Savannah.

An interesting story is told in the colonial records about a runaway. John Peter was a free Negro citizen of Dutch Curaçao in the West Indies. He and his trading boat had been captured in Spanish waters by a New England privateer. John Peter was sold as a slave but he escaped. He was captured off Tybee Island and jailed at Savannah. When he told the court he was a free man, the Savannah court refused to give him back to the man who had bought him. They believed him rather than his owner. John Peter was held in Savannah until he could prove his citizenship. When the governor of Curaçao sent certificates of his Dutch citizenship, John Peter was declared a free man. He was at liberty to return home to his trading business.

William Stephens had trouble with a runaway servant boy from London named Thomas Roberts. Young Roberts continually ran away and hid in the countryside or in town, stealing any food handy. He was sent to Stephens's plantation, Beaulieu, but he ran away. He ran away from another plantation farther from town and "was taken lurking under the house," where he had taken refuge after petty thieving. As a last resort Stephens sent him to work under Captain Kent, commander of the Augusta fort. The strict discipline must have been just what Thomas needed. He took to the drums and learned to play them. Several years later he joined the regiment at Frederica and was the best drummer in the regiment.

Growing Up to Self-Government

11

As mentioned in an earlier chapter, the colony of Georgia had presidents before it had governors. The charter of the Trustees was to last for twenty-one years. Before that period was over, the Trustees appointed a president for Georgia in 1741. This first president, William Stephens, also had some assistants but he did not have much power. The Trustees made the rules and decided most questions. They also furnished the money. The charter had made provision for a royal governor as in the other colonies but the Trustees never appointed one.

Here is another noteworthy fact about colonial Georgia. For the first twenty years of its existence the people had no voice whatsoever in their government. They did not vote for anyone, elect anyone or pay any taxes. They had their first royal governor in 1754. They had their first General Assembly with any legislative powers in 1755. Twenty years later rebellious Georgians decided to elect their own provincial congress. By the next year, 1775, Georgians had held their own independent provincial congress and had elected their own president, Archibald Bulloch. It is a remarkable story of growing up to self-government in a short time.

Why did the Trustees not give the people more voice in their affairs? From the rights of the charter the Trustees were in complete charge of the colony. Its primary purpose had been charitable and military. In the opinion of the Trustees the first people chosen to go over were poorly equipped for self-government until they had some success as frontiersmen. When Oglethorpe decided to go to Georgia, the Trustees were relieved. A trustee himself, Oglethorpe could act as director of the colony's affairs.

In the first years a strong, sensible guiding hand was essential. Oglethorpe felt, and had to act, as a father to the colonists. The Spanish war began to take more of his attention and he had less time for civil affairs. Finally, in 1743, Oglethorpe left Georgia for England. The colonists expected and hoped he would return but he never did. He had served Georgia faithfully for over ten years and had spent a great deal of his own fortune to preserve and protect it.

The Trustees had probably not thought too much about a government for Georgia. At first they expected it to be only a town settlement. The first officers they appointed were town officials. Their main job was to keep peace and hold court to settle small disputes. Bailiffs, constables and conservators of the peace were appointed but no mayor. As it happened, the Trustees' storekeeper, Thomas Causton, wielded a great deal of power, especially when Oglethorpe was not in Savannah. Since most people still depended on the Trustees for supplies, Causton became a little dictator because he issued food and supplies. He was removed for mismanagement in 1738.

The Trustees were much concerned by lack of news about Georgia. In 1737, William Stephens was sent from England to serve as secretary to the Trustees. He was to keep a daily

The seal of the Trustees of Georgia.

journal and write them about all the colony's activities. This he faithfully did until 1750 when James Habersham was appointed secretary. Stephens was well qualified. He was graduated from Cambridge and had served twenty years in Parliament. His good sense, ability and faithfulness made him the natural choice when the Trustees chose Georgia's first president.

The president and his four assistants had to refer many questions to the Trustees for decision. They were appointed by the Trustees to carry out the Trustees' orders or report if they did not. An important job of the president was acting as agent for Indian affairs. Stephens's age made him unable to continue as president, so in 1751, Henry Parker, the vice-president, acted as president. The last man appointed as president before Georgia became a royal colony was Patrick Graham.

Though all the colonists had agreed to the Trustees' rules before going to Georgia, they soon showed they were very human. They began to complain. They did not like the rule about owning land and wanted to own it outright without any strings. They wished to leave it to whom they pleased or sell it if they pleased. They wanted rum and they wanted slaves, both prohibited by the Trustees' laws. Some of them complained about the courts, the bailiffs, the storekeeper, the Trustees and Oglethorpe.

A group of colonists led by some Scotsmen who paid their own expenses brought serious discord to the colony. They were called malcontents. They petitioned the Trustees to change the landowning law and the law against slavery. Three of them wrote a book in which they brought serious charges against the Trustees and Oglethorpe and said the colony was on the verge of ruin. This happened about the time the Spaniards were threatening to invade Frederica. These malcontents were suspected by the Trustees of wanting to take over the lands granted to the colonists by getting the poorer ones in debt. One of them had a brother in the slave trade. By selling the colonists slaves on credit, they could soon own the land and control the colony.

Finally William Stephens's own son Thomas became leader of the malcontents. He turned against his father, the president, and carried the demands of the discontented to Parliament in London. The Trustees and Oglethorpe were accused before the House of Commons of mismanagement, misusing public money and abusing their civil power. Parliament thoroughly investigated these serious charges against a very respected, honorable group of men. The Trustees were completely cleared of charges and commended for their work. Thomas Stephens was called before Parliament and was publicly and "severely reprimanded by the Speaker for one-half hour on his knees." Thomas is said to have at first knelt on one knee but the Speaker thundered, "Both knees!"

Many colonists, especially those outside Savannah, did not petition for the right to own slaves. The Highlanders at Darien and the Salzburgers at Ebenezer sent petitions to the Trustees against slavery. Most of the colonists wanted the land law repealed so they could have their land at their disposal. The colony was not prospering. The planters could get no help. The indentured servants did not want to help with the necessary hard work and many ran away to South Carolina. Often the South Carolinians would not make them return. Fear of the Spanish, French and Indians kept out new settlers and caused many old ones to leave. In the other colonies they could own slaves and land without any restrictions.

Something had to be done. The Trustees finally legalized rum, ownership of land without restrictions and, with much reluctance, slavery. By then they were ready to give Georgia back to the king. Before this time they decided to have a practice assembly. The people from all over the settlements sent delegates. This assembly could pass no laws but it did make reports and suggestions. The Trustees wanted Georgia to have some practice in representative government before it became a crown colony. The Trustees gave up their charter to the king in 1752. It is remarkable that this distant government had done as well as it had.

Until the king had made ready the royal government, he asked the president and his assistants to remain in office. It was Patrick Graham who handed over control of Georgia to John Reynolds, the first royal governor. The governor was joyfully welcomed by the people at the riverside and that night bonfires and bellringing continued the celebration. The people of Georgia thought a new era had dawned. It was a new era of self-government but not the end of all their problems.

Under the royal governors the people had a voice in their government. The people elected representatives to a Commons House of Assembly. The colony was divided into parishes which served as both religious and legislative districts. The original ones were Christ Church (Savannah), St. Matthew (Ebenezer), St. George (Waynesboro), St. Paul (Augusta), St. Philip (Hardwick), St. John (Sunbury), St. Andrew (Darien), and St. James (Frederica). Later St. David, St. Patrick, St. Thomas, and St. Mary were added. There were usually about eighteen or twenty members of the Commons House. To be a member a colonist had to own land.

The Upper House of the General Assembly was also the Governor's Council. The Council was made up of the crown officers, such as the secretary and chief justice and from seven to twelve leading citizens. As a council these men advised and aided the governor. As the Upper House of the General Assembly they helped to make the laws of the colony. They were not elected as were the members of the Commons House. The members of the Governor's Council or Upper House were appointed by the king, often by the advice of the governor.

The real power in Georgia was in the hands of the governor. He was the civil and military ruler answerable to the King of England. He appointed officers, presided over the court of appeals, commanded the militia and controlled the land grants. He could convene, adjourn or dissolve the General Assembly. He could veto any bill. Since he was paid by the British government, the colonists had no power over him. A strong guiding hand on the scene was what Georgia seemed to need and this she received from the royal governors.

Governor Reynolds had the job of setting up and putting into operation Georgia's first real central government. Georgia was again in danger because of the French and Indian War. The colony was still very small and poor because settlers were afraid to come where there was no protection. Governor Reynolds increased the militia and planned forts. His experience as a naval captain tended to make him very autocratic and dictatorial to Georgia's new General Assembly and his own council. Also, he became very unpopular because he played favorites. Petitions were sent to the king by the colonists stating their grievances. Reynolds could not get the assembly to do as he wished, so he dissolved it. Finally the king recalled this naval captain who did not know how to be a politician. He left a Georgia which was full of dissension. The people of Georgia, however, had tested their power against arbitrary and despotic government.

The next governor, Henry Ellis, seemed to have a natural talent for getting along with everybody, including the Indians. He was an interesting man. He had been a natural scientist and an explorer. He had taken part in a sea expedition into the Hudson Straits to seek a new passage to the Pacific. He had written a book on his travels and been elected to the Royal Society of London. It is said he used to walk the streets of Savannah under a parasol which had a thermometer tied to it. This thermometer dangled before his nose so he could check the temperature. He thought the people in Savannah breathed the hottest air of any place on earth.

Henry Ellis gave Georgia his whole attention and good will and the people responded. He accomplished a great deal and restored harmony where Governor Reynolds had left violent discontent. We have already related an example of his success with the Indians. It is said that in one year he entertained about thirteen hundred Indians. He got forts built and repaired. Georgia's coast was defenseless against the raids of Spanish and French privateers. Governor Ellis fitted out a gunboat at his own expense to patrol and protect the coast.

Because of ill health, Governor Ellis asked to be released from his duties. When he left late in 1760 the whole colony grieved. The General Assembly publicly thanked him in a speech for the "zeal with which [he had] promoted and encouraged every measure tending to the public advantage." His terms of office had been successful and happy in every way for the "infant colony of Georgia."

James Wright was a happy choice to succeed Governor Ellis. He had experience in colonial government in South Carolina as attorney-general and in London as colonial agent. He was born in South Carolina and his wealth and interests were in America. The Georgia Commons House noted his "integrity and uprightness joyned with solid sense and sound judgment made him long esteemed in our neighboring province." It was under Governor Wright that the General Assembly became a sound lawmaking body. He respected the members as mature legislators and they responded by acting with maturity.

It was under Governor Wright that Georgia ceased to be an infant colony and began to prosper. There was a tremendous increase in trade, population and prosperity. This was principally due to a general peace and the end of danger to Georgia from French, Spanish and Indian foes. It was also due to continued wise government and cooperation between the governor and the General Assembly.

The peace of 1763, ending the French and Indian War, also brought Georgia new territory. Spain ceded Florida to Great Britain and the French withdrew west of the Mississippi. Georgia's border was extended south to the St. Mary's River and instead of the Spanish enemy Georgia had two new British colonies, East and West Florida, for neighbors. A treaty with the southern Indian tribes gave Georgia a large strip of territory between the Savannah and Ogeechee rivers and a coastal strip south to the St.

Mary's. The Indians could no longer find allies in the French and Spanish. In 1773 another treaty was made with the Indians ceding more lands to Georgia.

The land between the Altamaha and the St. Mary's Rivers was no longer a "debatable land" claimed by Spain and England. South Carolina now decided this territory belonged to it. This claim was based on an old grant made to South Carolina by Charles II. The South Carolina governor began to grant large tracts of this territory to a few South Carolinians. The Georgians were incensed. Many protests were sent to South Carolina and to England. Governor Wright protested to the British government how unfair it was that this land should be given to "strangers who never contributed one farthing or one hour's fatigue or hardship towards the support of the Province."

The British government supported Georgia's right to these lands. Peace and good available land brought streams of new settlers to Georgia. They came principally from Virginia, North Carolina and South Carolina and they settled in the uplands beyond the coastal regions. The coastal plantations flourished. Trade and prosperity increased. Harmony reigned between the people and the royal government until the British made the fatal mistake of passing the Stamp Act.

Liberty Boys and Loyal King's Men  12

The peace of 1763 which had started Georgia on the road to prosperity was a great one. Great Britain had conquered France and Spain but the war left England deep in debt. Great Britain thought the American colonies had greatly benefited from the victory so could help pay the debts. The Stamp Act was passed requiring that stamps or stamped papers be used for important legal documents. An unwise and uninformed king and ministry and Parliament were amazed at the outburst of protest in America. Virginia and Patrick Henry set up the cry "no taxation without representation," and Sons of Liberty sprang up in every colony. From Massachusetts to Georgia, the colonial post was kept busy with circular letters and protests.

Georgians also protested the Stamp Act. Loyal James Habersham, royal secretary of Georgia, thought it would ruin the colonies but he opposed violent resistance to it. The Sons of Liberty and the mobs which arose in the excitement were not so restrained. A foretaste of what was to happen in a little more than ten years occurred in October, 1765. On the anniversary of George III's accession to the throne, a number of people were in Savannah for the usual ceremonies and festivities. An unexpected and unloyal climax came at nightfall. An effigy of a stamp officer was paraded through the streets. There was a "very great tumult in the streets" and the effigy was hanged and burned to the approving shouts of a large crowd.

Peace and harmony were destroyed for colonial Georgia. Governor Wright would never more be without the Sons of Liberty and opposition to British policies. James Habersham wrote of the "terrible confusion" and said that he had been "threatened to be mobbed at night." Early in 1766 Governor Wright and British colonial authority were threatened by armed men determined to stop the use of stamps. The Rangers, led by Governor Wright armed with a musket, dispersed the group. Another larger group of several hundred came from the backcountry and marched on Savannah determined to take the stamps or shoot the governor. Again the governor was able to disperse them with the aid of troops and volunteers.

The violent reactions to the Stamp Act all over America should have opened British eyes. A very few British leaders and American colonial agents like Benjamin Franklin tried to tell them. They refused to listen. The causes of the American Revolution are very complex. But some understanding of British attitudes will help. To the British, the whole purpose of the colonies was the good of the mother country and the promotion of the empire. The colonies were to produce raw materials and buy manufactured goods only from England, which would protect them from enemies like France and Spain.

The British could not recognize the self-reliant, independent attitude that the Americans had developed. The frontier experience with its tendency toward equality and freedom was completely unknown to them. Many Britons thought Americans were somehow inferior, especially as soldiers, and would never resist British laws. The Americans were beginning to realize that these were the British attitudes. The restriction on colonial trade and increasing taxes were alarming. The Americans' petitions, protests and requests for representation in the British government were ignored. Some Americans gave up and sought independence as the only solution but others wished to remain British but have their own self-government.

This division of opinion among the American colonists made the break with England a civil war as well as a revolution. The colonists were divided among themselves as to the best way to get self-government. The Sons of Liberty or Liberty Boys led the fight for independence. Others remained loyal to the king but resisted the power of the British Parliament.

Georgia as a maturing colony now had more time to look up from its frontier labors. Georgians began to think of their relations with the other colonies and with England. Georgians were well aware of events in England and the other colonies. Benjamin Franklin became Georgia's colonial agent and kept them informed of events in London. They had a newspaper of their own and received them from other colonies and from England. A colonial postal service sped the letters and protests of colonial leaders and rebels to every colony. Attempts were made to involve Georgia in the united efforts of the colonies. It was invited to the Stamp Act Congress but sent no representative. South Carolina, a fiery leader for independence, undertook to aid and encourage the cause in Georgia.

More than any of the older colonies, Georgia had reason to remain loyal to England. From the beginning Georgia had been a favored colony. Parliament had contributed thousands of pounds sterling to its defense and support. Georgia now had peaceful borders and new lands to settle. Georgia was enjoying a real boom of prosperity for the first time so that boycotts and the closing of its ports could once again reduce it to a helpless condition. Still small in population, Georgia was far outnumbered by the neighboring Indian tribes and had to call on Britain for protection and help in furnishing goods to retain Indian friendships. The colony had a strong, wise governor whom the colonists respected as being truly interested in Georgia's progress.

All these things made Georgia very slow in demanding a complete break with England. Georgia's independent spirit showed itself in the gradual growth of power of the Commons House and in the continued activities of the Liberty Boys. Since the Crown paid the governor and other

The spirit of rebellion infected some of the youngest colonists who ridiculed the Loyalists.

officials, the assembly had less power in Georgia than in colonies where the governors were paid by the assemblies. The governor was able to keep control of Georgia's government. Governor Wright even felt secure enough to take a leave of nearly two years in London, from 1771 to 1773. He left James Habersham as acting governor.

The closing of the port of Boston by the British in 1774 because of the Boston Tea Party brought about strong reaction in Georgia. In July, a notice appeared in the *Georgia Gazette*. It requested all persons in the province to meet "at the liberty-pole at Tondee's tavern, in Savannah, on Wed., the 27th." They were to discuss the critical situation caused by this arbitrary act. The notice was signed by Noble W. Jones, Archibald Bulloch, John Houston and George Walton.

From this meeting came eight resolutions. These resolutions objected to recent actions of Parliament and affirmed the rights of the people. The group discussed sending delegates to the First Continental Congress but none were sent. Jonathan Bryan, a royal councillor, attended the meeting and then resigned from the Governor's Council. The meeting divided the colonists. Petitions and signatures were sent in from some towns and settlements voicing their disapproval of the resolutions.

Events began to move rapidly toward open defiance of British rule. Governor Wright was now powerless to stop it. He had no troops. Two significant statements from the *Georgia Gazette* in July, 1774, show the two minds of Georgians. One statement was, "The true interest of Britain and America are inseparable." The other told how at a recent coronation the principal diamond fell from the crown. It was found but the story continued that keepers of the crown should "not to be so careless about its principal diamond." Many Americans were aware that they, the Crown's principal diamond, might be lost from the crown.

Letters from Governor Wright to England at this time were full of warnings but England remained deaf.

While James Habersham and Noble Jones had grown old in the king's service, their sons became leaders of the rebellion. Since Georgia was a small colony, the leaders must have known each other well and often worked together. Contrary to the situation in other colonies, there was little personal animosity among the leaders. The rebel leaders made a conscious decision for liberty and freedom after despairing of anything but coercion from England.

Early in 1775 another meeting or provincial congress was held in Savannah. Noble W. Jones, John Houstoun and Archibald Bulloch were selected as delegates to the Second Continental Congress. They declined to go because they did not truly represent Georgia. Only five out of twelve parishes had sent delegates to Savannah. At this time the people of Darien had drawn up their own resolutions supporting Boston and the Continental Congress. One of these resolutions denounced slavery as "debasing part of our fellow creatures" and "laying the basis of that liberty we contend for on a very wrong foundation."

St. John's parish, home of the Midway congregation, had become impatient with Georgia. Like their New England forebears, the people of the parish were far along the independence road in their attitude toward England. Provoked that Georgia had sent no delegates to the First Continental Congress, St. John's parish sent a delegation to Charleston to form an alliance with South Carolina but South Carolina gave them no encouragement. The people of St. John's parish were offended and indignant with other Georgians for not supporting the Continental Congress. They elected their own delegate, Dr. Lyman Hall, to represent them at the congress. Dr. Hall attended the congress and took part in debates but he did not vote. Dr. Hall and other men from St. John's parish remained top revolutionary leaders.

Colonists drumming out a Tory.

Divisions and delays made Georgia seem lost to the revolutionary cause. The battles of Lexington and Concord turned the tide of opinion. The Liberty Boys began openly to take over the power of government. They broke open the powder magazine and made off with powder. They openly defied the king's birthday celebration by not attending and drinking toasts to Liberty under the liberty flag. For a while Savannah was almost under mob rule while the royal government was being undermined. Governor Wright pleaded for a warship and troops but none were sent. His mail was opened and stopped in Charleston. When no help came, the governor asked to be recalled to England.

Governor Wright reported to England that power had

been wrested from his hands. Five thousand pounds of powder and guns were seized and sent to South Carolina for the Liberty party. A British ship loaded with gunpowder was seized by the South Carolina and Georgia Liberty Boys. The Council of Safety was borrowing and issuing money, enlisting troops and directing military affairs. Gradually the council was taking over all civil and military control.

Though all Georgians were not in agreement, it became unsafe to disagree with the Liberty Boys. There were several cases of tarring and feathering. A pilot named Hopkins was taken from his house and tarred and feathered. He was made to stand with a candle in his hand in the square near the sundial in Savannah. Then he was carried about the streets for three hours in a cart. He had "behaved disrespectfully toward the Sons of Liberty." Another case of tarring and feathering occurred in Augusta. Thomas Brown was accused of activity against the rebels. He was taken to Augusta and received a similar treatment. The inhabitants had reason to regret this when Brown returned to Augusta as British military commander during the Revolutionary War.

Finally the British sent war vessels to Savannah. The Sons of Liberty took action. Joseph Habersham, son of James, went unarmed into a meeting of the Governor's Council. Placing his hand on the shoulder of Governor Wright, he pronounced him under arrest. Thus ended British rule in Georgia in January, 1776, until Savannah was recaptured by the British in 1778. The rebel leaders respected Governor Wright. When Wright fled to a British war ship they were relieved he had escaped safely.

The rebel leaders now made their government the real government of Georgia. They decided the head of Georgia should be president and commander-in-chief. Archibald

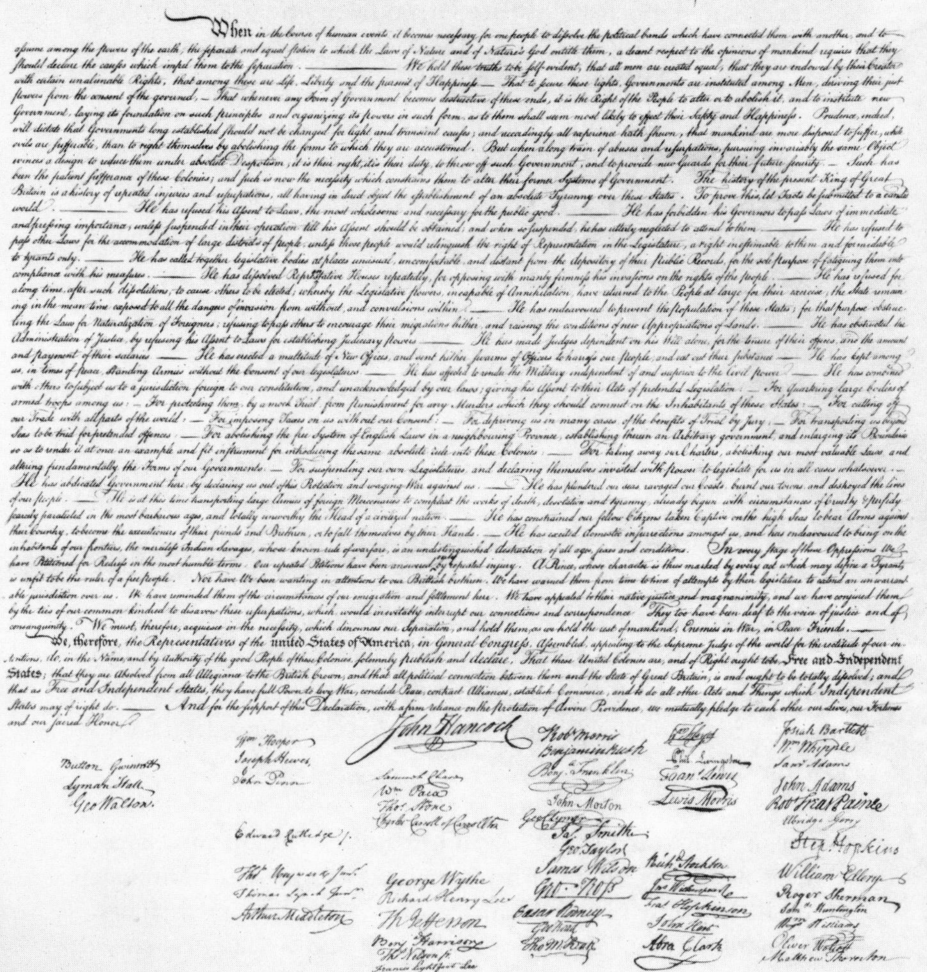

IN CONGRESS, JULY 4, 1776.

The unanimous Declaration of the thirteen united States of America,

When in the Course of human events it becomes necessary for one people to dissolve the political bands which have connected them with another, and to assume among the powers of the earth, the separate and equal station to which the Laws of Nature and of Nature's God entitle them, a decent respect to the opinions of mankind requires that they should declare the causes which impel them to the separation. —— We hold these truths to be self-evident, that all men are created equal, that they are endowed by their Creator with certain unalienable Rights, that among these are Life, Liberty and the pursuit of Happiness. — That to secure these rights, Governments are instituted among Men, deriving their just powers from the consent of the governed, — That whenever any Form of Government becomes destructive of these ends, it is the Right of the People to alter or to abolish it, and to institute new Government, laying its foundation on such principles and organizing its powers in such form, as to them shall seem most likely to effect their Safety and Happiness. Prudence, indeed, will dictate that Governments long established should not be changed for light and transient causes; and accordingly all experience hath shewn, that mankind are more disposed to suffer, while evils are sufferable, than to right themselves by abolishing the forms to which they are accustomed. But when a long train of abuses and usurpations, pursuing invariably the same Object evinces a design to reduce them under absolute Despotism, it is their right, it is their duty, to throw off such Government, and to provide new Guards for their future security. — Such has been the patient sufferance of these Colonies; and such is now the necessity which constrains them to alter their former Systems of Government. The history of the present King of Great Britain is a history of repeated injuries and usurpations, all having in direct object the establishment of an absolute Tyranny over these States. To prove this, let Facts be submitted to a candid world. —— He has refused his Assent to Laws, the most wholesome and necessary for the public good. —— He has forbidden his Governors to pass Laws of immediate and pressing importance, unless suspended in their operation till his Assent should be obtained; and when so suspended, he has utterly neglected to attend to them. —— He has refused to pass other Laws for the accommodation of large districts of people, unless those people would relinquish the right of Representation in the Legislature, a right inestimable to them and formidable to tyrants only. —— He has called together legislative bodies at places unusual, uncomfortable, and distant from the depository of their Public Records, for the sole purpose of fatiguing them into compliance with his measures. —— He has dissolved Representative Houses repeatedly, for opposing with manly firmness his invasions on the rights of the people. —— He has refused for a long time, after such dissolutions, to cause others to be elected; whereby the Legislative powers, incapable of Annihilation, have returned to the People at large for their exercise; the State remaining in the mean time exposed to all the dangers of invasion from without, and convulsions within. —— He has endeavoured to prevent the population of these States; for that purpose obstructing the Laws for Naturalization of Foreigners; refusing to pass others to encourage their migrations hither, and raising the conditions of new Appropriations of Lands. —— He has obstructed the Administration of Justice, by refusing his Assent to Laws for establishing Judiciary powers. —— He has made Judges dependent on his Will alone, for the tenure of their offices, and the amount and payment of their salaries. —— He has erected a multitude of New Offices, and sent hither swarms of Officers to harrass our people, and eat out their substance. —— He has kept among us, in times of peace, Standing Armies without the Consent of our legislatures. —— He has affected to render the Military independent of and superior to the Civil power. —— He has combined with others to subject us to a jurisdiction foreign to our constitution, and unacknowledged by our laws; giving his Assent to their Acts of pretended Legislation: —— For Quartering large bodies of armed troops among us: — For protecting them, by a mock Trial, from punishment for any Murders which they should commit on the Inhabitants of these States: — For cutting off our Trade with all parts of the world: — For imposing Taxes on us without our Consent: — For depriving us in many cases, of the benefits of Trial by Jury: — For transporting us beyond Seas to be tried for pretended offences: — For abolishing the free System of English Laws in a neighbouring Province, establishing therein an Arbitrary government, and enlarging its Boundaries so as to render it at once an example and fit instrument for introducing the same absolute rule into these Colonies: — For taking away our Charters, abolishing our most valuable Laws, and altering fundamentally the Forms of our Governments: — For suspending our own Legislatures, and declaring themselves invested with power to legislate for us in all cases whatsoever. —— He has abdicated Government here, by declaring us out of his Protection and waging War against us. —— He has plundered our seas, ravaged our Coasts, burnt our towns, and destroyed the lives of our people. —— He is at this time transporting large Armies of foreign Mercenaries to compleat the works of death, desolation and tyranny, already begun with circumstances of Cruelty & perfidy scarcely paralleled in the most barbarous ages, and totally unworthy the Head of a civilized nation. —— He has constrained our fellow Citizens taken Captive on the high Seas to bear Arms against their Country, to become the executioners of their friends and Brethren, or to fall themselves by their Hands. —— He has excited domestic insurrections amongst us, and has endeavoured to bring on the inhabitants of our frontiers, the merciless Indian Savages, whose known rule of warfare, is an undistinguished destruction of all ages, sexes and conditions. In every stage of these Oppressions We have Petitioned for Redress in the most humble terms: Our repeated Petitions have been answered only by repeated injury. A Prince, whose character is thus marked by every act which may define a Tyrant, is unfit to be the ruler of a free people. Nor have We been wanting in attentions to our Brittish brethren. We have warned them from time to time of attempts by their legislature to extend an unwarrantable jurisdiction over us. We have reminded them of the circumstances of our emigration and settlement here. We have appealed to their native justice and magnanimity, and we have conjured them by the ties of our common kindred to disavow these usurpations, which, would inevitably interrupt our connections and correspondence. They too have been deaf to the voice of justice and of consanguinity. We must, therefore, acquiesce in the necessity, which denounces our Separation, and hold them, as we hold the rest of mankind, Enemies in War, in Peace Friends. ——

We, therefore, the Representatives of the united States of America, in General Congress, Assembled, appealing to the Supreme Judge of the world for the rectitude of our intentions, do, in the Name, and by Authority of the good People of these Colonies, solemnly publish and declare, That these United Colonies are, and of Right ought to be Free and Independent States; that they are Absolved from all Allegiance to the British Crown, and that all political connection between them and the State of Great Britain, is and ought to be totally dissolved; and that as Free and Independent States, they have full Power to levy War, conclude Peace, contract Alliances, establish Commerce, and to do all other Acts and Things which Independent States may of right do. —— And for the support of this Declaration, with a firm reliance on the protection of divine Providence, we mutually pledge to each other our Lives, our Fortunes and our sacred Honor.

Button Gwinnett
Lyman Hall
Geo Walton.

Wm Hooper
Joseph Hewes,
John Penn

Edward Rutledge 1.

Thos Heyward Junr.
Thomas Lynch Junr.
Arthur Middleton

John Hancock

Samuel Chase
Wm Paca
Thos Stone
Charles Carroll of Carrollton

George Wythe
Richard Henry Lee
Th Jefferson
Benja Harrison
Thos Nelson jr.
Francis Lightfoot Lee
Carter Braxton

Robt Morris
Benjamin Rush
Benja Franklin
John Morton
Geo Clymer
Jas Smith.
Geo. Taylor
James Wilson
Geo. Ross
Caesar Rodney
Geo Read
Tho M:Kean

Wm Floyd
Phil. Livingston
Frans Lewis
Lewis Morris

Richd Stockton
Jno Witherspoon
Fras Hopkinson
John Hart
Abra Clark

Josiah Bartlett
Wm Whipple
Saml Adams
John Adams
Robt Treat Paine
Elbridge Gerry
Step. Hopkins
William Ellery
Roger Sherman
Samel Huntington
Wm Williams
Oliver Wolcott
Matthew Thornton

Button Gwinett, Lyman Hall and George Walton signed the Declaration of Independence in the far left column.

Bulloch was again elected. The old leaders, James Habersham and Noble Jones were dead. Others had left or were banished. The sons of original colonists and people who were born or brought up in America took control. They believed in America's ability, its power and its future.

With the signing of the Declaration of Independence there was no turning back. The three Georgians who signed were George Walton, Button Gwinnett and Lyman Hall. The news of the Declaration of Independence reached Georgia on August 10, 1776. President Bulloch called for the people to assemble to hear the news. The following account comes from the *Universal Intelligencer* for 1776. The Declaration was read to a great crowd in the Assembly House Square. Then all proceeded to the Liberty Pole where it was read again. The procession, made up of the president, council, the military, and the citizens, gathered for the final reading at the battery at the Trustees' Garden. The cannon were fired. The president and council, Colonel Lachlan McIntosh, commander of Georgia's battalion, and others dined under the cedar trees and drank toasts to the United States. Chief among the evening festivities was a mock funeral procession. There was a military guard, drums, fifes and a huge crowd of people. King George III was buried in effigy before the court house with the following words:

> For as much as George the Third, of Great Britain, hath most flagrantly violated his coronation oath, and trampled upon the constitution of our country, and the sacred rights of mankind; we therefore commit his political existence to the ground—tyranny to the grave—and oppression to eternal infamy; in sure and certain hope that he will never obtain a resurrection to rule again over these United States of America. But, my friends and fellow citizens, let us not be sorry as men without hope, for Tyrants that thus depart.

Rather let us remember America is free and independent; that she is, and will be, with the blessing of the Almighty, great among the nations of the earth. Let this encourage us in well-doing, to fight for our rights and privileges, our wives and children, for all that is near and dear unto us. May God give us his blessing, and let all the people say, AMEN.

Bibliography

ABBOTT, WILLIAM WRIGHT. *The Royal Governors of Georgia, 1754–1775*. Chapel Hill: University of North Carolina Press, 1959.

BESANT, SIR WALTER. *London in the Eighteenth Century*. London: A. & C. Black, 1925.

BOLTON, HERBERT and ROSS, MARY. *The Debatable Land, a Sketch of the Anglo-Spanish Contest for the Georgia Country*. Berkeley: University of California Press, 1925.

CANDLER, A. D., and KNIGHT, L. L., eds. *Colonial Records of Georgia*. 26 vols. Atlanta, Georgia: Franklin Printing Co., 1904–1916. Additional volumes in manuscript form are available from the Georgia State Department of Archives.

COLEMAN, KENNETH. *The American Revolution in Georgia, 1763–1789*. Athens: University of Georgia Press, 1958.

CORRY, JOHN PITTS. *Indian Affairs in Georgia, 1732–1756*. Philadelphia: 1936.

DONNAN, ELIZABETH, ed. *Documents Illustrative of the History of the Slave Trade to America*. vol. 2, eighteenth century. Washington: Carnegie Institution of Washington, 1930–1935.

EGMONT, JOHN PERCEVAL, 1st earl of, 1683–1748. *The Journal of the Earl of Egmont, 1732–1738*, ed. by ROBERT G. MC PHERSON. Athens: University of Georgia Press, 1962.

EGMONT, JOHN PERCEVAL, 1st earl of, 1683–1748. *Manuscripts of the Earl of Egmont. Diary of Viscount Percival afterwards first Earl of Egmont*. London: H. M. Stationery Office. 1920–1923. 3 vols.

ETTINGER, AMOS A., *James Edward Oglethorpe: Imperial Idealist*. Oxford: The Clarendon Press, 1936.

FLANDERS, RALPH BETTS. *Plantation Slavery in Georgia*. Chapel Hill: University of North Carolina Press, 1933.

FLEMING, BERRY, comp. *The Autobiography of a Colony, The First Half-Century of Augusta, Georgia*. Athens: University of Georgia Press, 1957.

FRIES, ADELAIDE L. *The Moravians in Georgia, 1735–1740.* Baltimore: Genealogical Pub. Co., 1967.

GEORGIA HISTORICAL SOCIETY. *Collections.* vols. 1–7, 13.

GORDON, PETER. *Journal, 1732–1735,* ed. by E. MERTON COULTER. Athens: University of Georgia Press, 1963.

HARPER, FRANCIS, ed. *Travels of William Bartram,* naturalists edition, edited with commentary and an annotated index. New Haven: Yale University Press, 1958.

JONES, CHARLES C. *History of Georgia.* 2 vols. Boston: Houghton Mifflin, 1883.

MC CAIN, JAMES ROSS. *Georgia as a Proprietary Province.* Boston: Richard Badger, c. 1917.

SAYE, ALBERT B. *New Viewpoints in Georgia History.* Athens: University of Georgia Press, 1943.

STEPHENS, WILLIAM. *The Journal of William Stephens,* ed. by E. MERTON COULTER. Athens: University of Georgia Press, 1958–1959. 2 vols.

STROBEL, P. A. *The Salzburgers and Their Descendants.* Athens: University of Georgia Press, 1953. Reprint of original edition, 1855.

TEMPLE, SARAH B. and COLEMAN, KENNETH. *Georgia Journeys.* Athens: University of Georgia Press, 1961.

TUNIS, EDWIN. *Indians.* Cleveland: World Publishing Co., 1959.

VER STEEG, CLARENCE L., ed. *A True and Historical Narrative of the Colony of Georgia.* Athens: University of Georgia Press, 1960.

Important Dates

1540—Hernando De Soto visits the territory now called Georgia.

1566—Pedro de Menendez establishes the first Spanish fort on St. Catherine's Island in the district of Guale.

1702—Spanish withdraw their forts and missions from Guale (Georgia) to the St. John's River.

1721—The British build Fort King George at the mouth of the Altamaha River.

1732—On June 9 the Charter of the Colony of Georgia is granted to the Trustees for Establishing the Colony of Georgia in America by King George II of Great Britain.

1732—On November 17 the first colonists for Georgia sail from Gravesend on the ship *Ann.* They are accompanied by James Oglethorpe.

1733—The colonists arrive at Yamacraw Bluff on the Savannah River to spend their first night on Georgia soil. This date was February 1, Old Style; February 12, New Style.

1733—The Creek chiefs sign a treaty with Oglethorpe in May, granting the English the land between the Savannah and Altamaha Rivers from the Atlantic Ocean to the head of the tidewater.

1734—The first Salzburger settlers arrive at Savannah and select the town site of Ebenezer. Oglethorpe sails to England accompanied by Tomo-chi-chi, Toonahowie and other Indians.

1735—A group of Highlanders leave Inverness, Scotland, for Georgia to settle at Darien on the Altamaha River.

1736—Oglethorpe returns to Georgia accompanied by John and Charles Wesley and a large group of colonists for the new town of Frederica.

1737—William Stephens, the Trustees' secretary, arrives at Savannah to begin his duties. John Wesley leaves Georgia for England in December.

1739—The War of Jenkins' Ear breaks out between England and Spain.

1740—Oglethorpe attacks St. Augustine. George Whitefield founds the Bethesda Orphanage.

1741—William Stephens is appointed Georgia's first president.

1742—Spain invades Georgia. The Spanish are defeated by Ogle-Thorpe and his troops at the Battle of Bloody Marsh, St. Simon's Island.

1752—The Trustees relinquish their charter and Georgia becomes a royal colony.

1754—Georgia gets her first royal governor, Captain John Reynolds.

1755—The first General Assembly of Georgia with legislative powers is convened in Savannah.

1757—Henry Ellis becomes the royal governor of Georgia after the recall of Governor Reynolds.

1760—James Wright becomes the third royal governor of Georgia after the retirement of Henry Ellis.

1763—By the Treaty of Paris, Georgia's territory is extended to the St. Mary's River. First publication of the *Georgia Gazette.*

1765—Georgians react against the Stamp Act. Sons of Liberty are organized.

1773—The Creeks cede new lands to Georgia.

1774—A meeting of the citizens of Georgia is called in Savannah to consider the critical situation of the American colonies.

1775—A Council of Safety is formed in Savannah. The Provincial Congress meets in Savannah. Archibald Bulloch is elected president and delegates are selected to the Continental Congress.

1776—Governor Wright is arrested by the Council of Safety, later escaping on a British warship.

—Georgia adopts a new form of government. The new head of government to be called president and commander-in-chief. Bulloch is elected president.

—Declaration of Independence is celebrated in Georgia in August when news reaches Savannah.

Places To Visit

Among the many historic sites in Georgia which readers of this book will find of interest are:

AUGUSTA

AUGUSTA MUSEUM. 540 Telfair Street. An interesting collection of Indian artifacts and other historical exhibits, open to adults and children over ten. Tuesday-Saturday, 2–5 P.M.; closed Christmas and New Year's Day. Admission free.

MEADOW GARDEN. 1320 Nelson Street. A late eighteenth-century house that was the residence of George Walton, who signed the Declaration of Independence. The house is fully restored with furniture, paintings and exhibits of colonial clothing. Admission 50¢; under twelve, free.

SITE OF FORT AUGUSTA. Corner of Reynolds and Washington Streets. In the churchyard of St. Paul's Episcopal Church stands a cross marking the site of Fort Augusta, built under the supervision of James Oglethorpe.

MIDWAY

MIDWAY CHURCH. Built by the Puritans from Massachusetts in 1792, this white clapboard building is similar to colonial New England meeting houses. The first church was a log structure built in 1754.

MIDWAY COLONIAL MUSEUM. On U.S. 17. The museum contains exhibits of colonial furnishings and documents. There is a library of early records and history. Open May through October, Monday-Thursday, Saturday, 9 A.M.–5:30 P.M.; November through April, 9 A.M.–5 P.M.; all year, Sunday, 2–5 P.M. Admission 50¢, under sixteen, 10¢.

MACON

OCMULGEE NATIONAL MONUMENT. One mile south of Macon at the junction of U.S. 80 and U.S. 129. A large, scientifically excavated

Indian site showing the remains of ten thousand years of Indian settlements. The Creeks inhabited this area when the Europeans settled Georgia. The museum at the site contains exhibits showing Indian history. Open Monday-Saturday, 8:30 A.M.–5:30 P.M; Sunday, 9 A.M.–5:30 P.M; closed Christmas Day and New Year's Day. Admission 50¢; fifteen years and under, free.

ST. SIMON'S ISLAND

FORT FREDERICA NATIONAL MONUMENT. Excavation of Fort Frederica and the town of Frederica, founded under the supervision of James Oglethrope in 1734. The Visitor's Center contains exhibits dealing with the town's life and history. Open daily May 30–Labor Day, 8 A.M.–7 P.M; remainder of the year, 8 A.M.–5 P.M. Admission free.

SAVANNAH

THE PINK HOUSE. 23 Abercorn Street. This handsome Georgian Colonial house, built in 1771, is now a restaurant.

TRUSTEES' GARDEN SITE. East Broad Street. Site of the ten-acre Trustees' experimental garden. Fort Wayne was built on this site in 1762. An inn for visiting seamen built in 1734 has been restored and is now a restaurant.

WRIGHT SQUARE. Bull Street between State and York Streets. One of the city's fifty-two small parks, it was laid out in 1733. The Tomo-chi-chi Marker in the southeast corner of the Square honors the Yamacraw chief who befriended Oglethorpe and the first settlers.

Times and admission prices subject to change.

Index